CONGRESSIONAL CHALLENGERS

In this book, Costas Panagopoulos examines patterns of candidate emergence in congressional elections over the past five decades—specifically, the quality of challengers who seek to unseat U.S. House incumbents, as measured by prior political experience. Panagopoulos demonstrates that fewer and fewer experienced challengers have tossed their hats into the ring since the early 1970s. Inexperienced candidates often face electoral challengers that are difficult to overcome. Looking at factors including campaign spending, district-level partisan composition, and institutional reforms such as term limits, Panagopoulos evaluates explanations and consequences for these developments over time. He points to important implications for the study of congressional elections and democracy in the United States, including reforms in recruitment and candidate selection strategies to heighten electoral competition and ultimately, to enhance democratic representation in Congress. For students and scholars of the U.S. Congress and elections, this book addresses public concerns about representation as well.

Costas Panagopoulos is Professor of Political Science and Chair of the Department of Political Science at Northeastern University.

PRAISE FOR *CONGRESSIONAL CHALLENGERS*

"*Congressional Challengers* is a rigorous empirical analysis of the causes and characteristics of the decline in the supply of experienced challengers in congressional elections. It is a valuable and unique discussion of the decline of competitiveness and quality challengers in congressional elections and the consequences for Congress and our democracy."

James A. Thurber, *American University*

"The study of congressional challenger quality has a long and rich history, and with good reason: challenger quality has been shown to be an important determinant of outcomes in congressional elections. Costas Panagopoulos has written an extraordinary book that makes an invaluable contribution to this rich scholarly literature. Panagopoulos traces patterns of challenger quality over time from 1972 to 2018, finding that there has been a decline in challenger quality in incumbent races (but not in open-seat races). He considers an impressive array of possible explanations for this pattern, finding that it is the increase in incumbent electoral strength in their home districts that has the dominant effect in discouraging high-quality candidates to challenge incumbents. This central finding has important normative implications for the health of our American republic. *Congressional Challengers* is an important, must-read book for those interested in congressional elections and, even more broadly, those interested in understanding the workings of our American democracy."

James C. Garand, *Louisiana State University*

"It is difficult to overstate the importance of challenger quality to understanding the outcomes of U.S. legislative elections. Panagopoulos has significantly expanded our knowledge of this important feature of American politics with a careful and exhaustive analysis. The finding that challenger quality has declined over time, and that this is due to decreases in the competitiveness of races rather than increases in campaign costs, constitutes a major contribution, making this book a must read for anyone interested in elections, representation, and the overall health of American democracy."

Gregory Wawro, *Columbia University*

"Costas Panagopoulos presents an important study of U.S. congressional elections. Panagopoulos shows that the quality of candidates that challenge congressional incumbents has declined since 1972. Using careful empirical analyses that incorporate different theoretical explanations, Panagopoulos demonstrates that this decline in challenger quality is explained by district competitiveness: As congressional districts more heavily favor one party or the other, high quality candidates choose not to challenge the incumbents of those districts, thus weakening a link in the chain of democratic representation. *Congressional Challengers* deserves the close attention of scholars of elections."

Jay Goodliffe, *Brigham Young University*

"In this book, Costas Panagopoulos documents the decline from 1972 to 2018 in the supply of high-quality congressional challengers. What makes this book special and noteworthy is that it goes beyond the standard academic explanation that high-quality challengers are strategic actors who run for congressional office when incumbents are vulnerable. Panagopoulos makes a major contribution to the academic literature by presenting results that show there is more to this story, specifically that declines in competitiveness, defined as the share of the two-party vote earned by the incumbent's party presidential candidate, are a major factor in understanding this development. These convincing and important new findings shed light on a subject of interest to anybody who studies or cares about congressional elections in the United States."

Peter L. Francia, *East Carolina University*

CONGRESSIONAL CHALLENGERS

Candidate Quality in U.S. Elections to Congress

Costas Panagopoulos

NEW YORK AND LONDON

Cover image: © Shutterstock

First published 2022
by Routledge
605 Third Avenue, New York, NY 10158

and by Routledge
2 Park Square, Milton Park, Abingdon, Oxon, OX14 4RN

Routledge is an imprint of the Taylor & Francis Group, an informa business

© 2022 Taylor & Francis

The right of Costas Panagopoulos to be identified as author of this work has been asserted in accordance with sections 77 and 78 of the Copyright, Designs and Patents Act 1988.

All rights reserved. No part of this book may be reprinted or reproduced or utilised in any form or by any electronic, mechanical, or other means, now known or hereafter invented, including photocopying and recording, or in any information storage or retrieval system, without permission in writing from the publishers.

Trademark notice: Product or corporate names may be trademarks or registered trademarks, and are used only for identification and explanation without intent to infringe.

Library of Congress Cataloging-in-Publication Data
Names: Panagopoulos, Costas, author.
Title: Congressional challengers : candidate quality in U.S. elections to Congress / Costas Panagopoulos.
Description: New York, NY : Routledge, 2022. | Includes bibliographical references and index.
Identifiers: LCCN 2021034726 (print) | LCCN 2021034727 (ebook) | ISBN 9781138057876 (hardback) | ISBN 9780367754419 (paperback) | ISBN 9781315164649 (ebook)
Subjects: LCSH: Political candidates--United States. | Political campaigns--United States. | United States. Congress. House--Elections. | Opposition (Political science)--United States. | Incumbency (Public officers)--United States.
Classification: LCC JK1976 .P323 2022 (print) | LCC JK1976 (ebook) | DDC 324.973/092--dc23
LC record available at https://lccn.loc.gov/2021034726
LC ebook record available at https://lccn.loc.gov/2021034727

ISBN: 978-1-138-05787-6 (hbk)
ISBN: 978-0-367-75441-9 (pbk)
ISBN: 978-1-315-16464-9 (ebk)

DOI: 10.4324/9781315164649

Typeset in Bembo
by Deanta Global Publishing Services, Chennai, India

CONTENTS

Dedication and Acknowledgements	ix
List of figures	x
List of tables	xii

1	Dynamics of Challenger Quality: Introduction	1
2	Challenger Quality—Conceptualization and Measurement	25
3	Explaining Challenger Quality: Hypotheses and Methodology	41
4	Money and Challenger Quality	48
5	Candidate Quality and Campaign Communications Strategies	58
6	Movin' On Up: The Impact of State Legislative Term Limits on Candidate Quality in U.S. House Elections, 1972–2018	68
7	States of Ambition: Aggregate Challenger Quality in the U.S. by State, 1972–2018	77
8	Explaining the Decline in Challenger Quality, 1972–2018	83
9	Implications: Challenger Quality, Incumbency Advantage, and Democracy in America	109

10 Conclusion   119

References   *123*
Appendix   *129*
Index   *131*

DEDICATION AND ACKNOWLEDGEMENTS

I dedicate this book to my parents—George (1943-2009) and Vasiliki Panagopoulos.

Even as the only formal educational training they earned in Greece was limited to elementary school, my parents instilled in me a deep appreciation for education and knowledge. Their sacrifices and their example are a daily inspiration, and I miss my father every day.

Like many projects, this book began as a dissertation in the Department of Politics at NYU. As such, it benefitted greatly from invaluable input from Jonathan Nagler, my lead advisor who challenged me to expand my scholarly abilities and technical skills, and Anna Harvey. Robert S. Erikson, also a member of my committee, trekked frequently to Greenwich Village from atop Morningside Heights to discuss the project over many delectable meals. He was a faithful mentor, and his boundless intellectual curiosity remains an inspiration. He is a scholar and a gentleman, and I am proud to consider him my friend.

I also acknowledge Richard Fleisher for his support and encouragement, first as one of my graduate teachers, then as an outside reader on my dissertation committee, and finally as my colleague in the Department of Political Science at Fordham for over a decade. His mentorship and friendship remain among the most treasured gifts academia has offered me to date.

I also thank Gary Jacobson, for generously providing data and for insights about the project overall, and Tim Fraser, Zacharias Dupaix, and Samuel Gass for research assistance.

FIGURES

1.1 Reelection Rates for Incumbents, U.S. House (1972–2018)   6
1.2 Average Challenger Voteshares by Experience (1972–2018)   8
1.3 Proportion of Incumbents Facing Experienced Challengers, U.S. House, (1972–2018)   14
1.4 Proportion of Experienced Challengers by Party, U.S. House (1972–2018)   15
1.5 Proportion of Experienced Challengers, U.S. Senate Elections (1972–2012)   17
1.6 Proportion of Experienced Challengers, House and Senate (1972–2012)   18
1.7 Proportion of Open Seat HR Races with at Least One Experienced Candidate (General Election) (1972–2018)   19
1.8 Proportion of Open Seat HR Races with Two Experienced Candidates (General Election) (1972–2018)   19
1.9 Proportion of Open Seat HR Races with One Experienced Candidate (General Election) (1972–2018)   20
1.10 Proportion of Open Seat HR Races by Experienced Candidate, by Party (General Election) (1972–2018)   21
4.1 Average Campaign Expenditures by Candidate (General Election) (1972–2018)   49
4.2 Average Television Advertising Costs (CPM) for Various Times, 1972–2012   51
4.3 Cable TV Penetration, 1972–2014   52
4.4 Total Spending on Political TV Advertising, Spot/Local, 1972–2014   52

4.5	Average Campaign Expenditures by Candidate and Challenger Types (1972–2018)	53
4.6	Proportion of Total PAC Contributions to U.S. House Candidates: Candidates by type (1978–2014)	54
4.7	Proportion of Challengers with Competitive Expenditure Levels (1972–2018)	55
4.8	Proportion of Challengers with Competitive Expenditure Levels by Type (1972–2018)	56
4.9	Proportion of Challengers with Competitive Expenditure Levels (at Various Levels) (1972–2018)	57
5.1	Comparison of Means by Candidate Status for each Ad Attribute	62
5.2	Incumbents' Communication Strategies by Opponent Type	64
7.1	Challenger Quality Dynamics by State (1972–2018) (Map)	78
8.1	Probabilities of Experienced Challenger by Challenger Spending	95
8.2	Probabilities of Experienced Challenger by Incumbent Party Strength	96
8.3	Incumbent Party Strength in District (Mean), 1972–2018	98
9.1	Estimates of Total Incumbency Advantage in U.S. House Elections (1974–2018)	115
9.2	Direct and Indirect Effects (Scare-off and Quality) in House Elections (1974–2018)	116

TABLES

2.1	Quality—Conceptualization and Measurement	27
2.2	Emergence of Quality Challenger—Summary	35
4.1	Average Campaign Expenditures U.S. House (1972–2018)	50
6.1	Mean Levels of Aggregate Challenger Quality Given Limits in Place vs. No Limits by State (1972–2018)	71
6.2	Mean Levels of Aggregate Challenger Quality by States with Limits vs. States without Limits (1996–2018)	72
6.3	Proportion of Challengers who were Previously State Legislators Given Limits in Places vs. No Limits By State (1972–2018)	73
6.4	Proportion of Open Seat Races with At Least One High-Quality Candidate, Given Limits in Places vs. No Limits By State (1972–2018)	74
6.5	Proportion of Open Seat Races with At Least One Candidate Who Was Previously State Legislator, Given Limits in Places vs. No Limits By State (1972–2018)	75
6.6	State Legislative Term Limits and Re-election Rates (U.S. House)	76
7.1	Challenger Quality Dynamics by State (1972–2018)	78
7.2	High-Quality Challengers by Level of State Legislative Professionalism	79
7.3	High-Quality Challengers by Level of Party Competition	79
7.4	High-Quality Challengers by State Legislative Term Limits	79
7.5	State-level Institutional Determinants of Proportion of Experienced Challengers (2012)	81

8.1	Summary Statistics	84
8.2	Probability of an Experienced Challenger, 1974–2018 (Probit)	88
8.3	Probability of an Experienced Challenger, by Party, 1974–2018 (Probit)	90
8.4	Probability of an Experienced Challenger, 1974–2012 (Probit)	92
8.5	Probability of an Experienced Challenger, by Party, 1974–2018 (Probit)	93
8.6	Expected Probability of Experienced Challenger for selected values of Lagged Challenger Spending and Incumbent Party Strength in the Districts	97
8.7	Probability of an Experienced Challenger, 1974–2018	104
8.8	Proportion of Experienced Challengers, by Levels of Incumbent Margin of Victory and Challenger Spending in Previous Election	106
8.9	Expected Probability of Experienced Challengers for selected values of Lagged Challenger Spending and Lagged Incumbent Margin of Victory Given varying Lagged Incumbent Spending	106
9.1	Decomposition of Incumbency Advantage in U.S. House Elections (1974–2018)	114
9.2	Rate of Growth in Direct and Indirect Effects in House Elections (1974–2018)	116
A7.1	Proportion of High-Quality Challengers (Avg., 1972–2018) and Change in Overall Proportion of High-Quality Challengers (1972–2018) by State	130

1
DYNAMICS OF CHALLENGER QUALITY

Introduction

> *Decide on some imperfect Somebody and you will win, because the truest truism in politics is: You can't beat Somebody with Nobody.*
>
> —*William Safire*

Elections, it is commonly claimed, *are* the heart of democracy. More accurately, democracy relies on *meaningful* elections that offer voters realistic choices. Developments in contemporary congressional elections suggest this may be an elusive ideal in America. Congressional contests appear to be increasingly lopsided over the past few decades, disproportionately favoring incumbents with near-perfect protection from electoral defeat. Weak opposition has become a popular explanation often cited to explain incumbents' strong showing at the polls. To measure opposition strength, political scientists have developed the notion of challenger quality, which, in the simplest formulation, is an indicator of challengers' prior political experience. Studies have repeatedly revealed that strong challengers—those with prior elective experience—engage incumbents in more balanced contests. In lofty terms, quality challengers may be the best defense citizens have against meaningless congressional contests.

Challenger quality has steadily declined over the past three decades. In 1972, nearly one in three challengers in contested elections for the U.S. House of Representatives had prior political experience as an elected official. By 1990, the proportion of politically experienced challengers had dropped over half, to one in eight. Ten years later, in 2000, only slightly more than one in five congressional challengers had previously served in public office and remained about the same

2 Dynamics of Challenger Quality

through 2014. Despite this modest uptick, challenger quality overall systematically declined between 1972 and 2018.

In this book I document the decline in the supply of experienced challengers between 1972 and 2018. I then turn my attention to the more complex task of explaining the decline in quality I observe. At first glance, this decline may appear reasonable, given that rational politicians, evaluating prospects for victory, simply opt out of challenging incumbents, preferring instead to wait for open seat races. Armed with increasingly abundant, accessible, and accurate advice and information about electoral prospects, potential challengers may be acting more strategically over time by waiting to mount campaigns in races that do not include an incumbent.

Notwithstanding this possibility, I demonstrate that the overall supply of experienced candidates in open seat races has not increased during the period of this study while challenger quality in contested races against incumbents has declined. In fact, there has been no appreciable change in the overall proportion of experienced candidates in open seat races for the U.S. House between 1972 and 2018. Thus, the "rational politicians" explanation alone does not sufficiently account for the decline in challenger quality we observe. The puzzle of dwindling challenger quality persists, and it is primarily this puzzle that this study aims to resolve.

I propose that declining competitiveness explains a good part of the decline in challenger quality observed. For the purposes of my study, I define "competitiveness" as the partisan composition of the congressional district as determined by the share of the two-party vote earned by the incumbent's party presidential candidate in the most recent presidential election. I also consider that rising campaign costs help to explain the decline in quality, but I find scant empirical evidence to support this idea in my analyses.

The results of the analyses I present in the following chapters provide strong empirical support to confirm that declining competitiveness explains nearly all of the decline in quality.

In the remainder of this chapter, I present a more detailed description of challenger quality and its measurement. I also describe the dynamics of challenger quality between 1972 and 2018, and demonstrate the decline in challenger quality between 1972 and 2018. Additionally, I show that quality in open seat races during this period has not changed. I begin by providing an overview of the chapters that follow as a roadmap for the argument and the analyses I conduct to resolve the puzzle of dwindling quality in U.S. House elections.

Organization

What explains the decline in challenger quality we observe between 1972 and 2018?

The chapters that follow aim to provide an answer to this question. I begin in Chapter 2 by reviewing the rich scholarly literature that has addressed questions related to challenger quality in congressional elections. After accepting the findings of early work that identified quality as a powerful determinant of electoral outcomes, scholars' main pursuits in this area have revolved around either refining measurement of quality or identifying the determinants of quality. Chapter 2 summarizes and evaluates the findings of the main works, emphasizing results and methodological issues that are most relevant to this study.

In Chapter 3, I develop a theoretical model and hypotheses about the effects of a variety of factors on challenger quality. I explain that my argument assumes politicians to be rational, strategic actors who evaluate the political environment in seeking to make decisions that maximize utility. Based on this theoretical foundation, and along with the theoretical guidance described in the previous chapter, I expect challenger quality to be related to campaign costs, competitiveness, majority status in the legislature, and state legislative term limits. I also develop theories about why I believe we observe a decline in overall quality during this period. I propose that rising campaign costs and diminishing competitiveness in elections for the U.S. House explain the decline in quality we observe.

Chapter 4 presents descriptive details about campaign costs and spending in congressional elections between 1972 and 2018. I show that campaign costs have increased significantly for all categories of candidates. I also demonstrate that challengers, especially inexperienced or low-quality challengers, are systematically disadvantaged with respect to campaign finances. I assert that the developments in campaign costs during this period should help explain the downward trend in quality we observe, a proposition tested empirically in subsequent analyses.

In Chapter 5, I exploit available data about congressional candidates' television advertising strategies in the 2004 election cycle to compare content and tone by candidate type. The analyses suggest incumbents' communication strategies are slightly more in line with strategies pursued by high-quality challengers, but inexperienced challengers' strategies are not dissimilar. These findings challenge assertions that experienced challengers' communications strategies differ qualitatively from their inexperienced counterparts and call into question claims that such differences account for imbalances at the ballot box.

I proceed to examine the impact of term limits on challenger quality, an institutional feature I believe to be an important factor that has been largely overlooked in the extant literature. Chapter 6 presents an in-depth analysis of state legislative term limits, expands on the rationale behind my expectations about state legislative term limits' effect on quality, and reviews additional literature that focuses on state legislative term limits. I also conduct some basic analyses to explore the impact of limits on quality. I explain that, although state legislative term limits is a relatively new political phenomenon, there is adequate data available to advance some initial analyses that take advantage of the natural experiment that the adoption of state legislative term limits in some states (and not others) provides. The findings of these initial analyses are presented in Chapter 6. I conclude from these preliminary analyses that state legislative term limits likely exert a positive effect on challenger quality, but the empirical evidence to support this conclusion is rather weak and refuted by the more rigorous analyses presented in later chapters.

Chapter 7 aggregates challenger quality to the state level and investigates the dynamics of overall quality across states between 1972 and 2018. I describe the patterns I observe across states and suggest possible explanations that may account for these patterns. Specifically, I argue that two additional (besides state legislative term limits), state-level factors may impact challenger quality: State legislative professionalism and party competition. I conduct some initial analyses about the effect of these factors. I find that none of the above factors exerts any statistically significant effects on quality. I will, however, include these variables in multivariate models I estimate in Chapter 8 to conduct more systematic tests of the impact of these state-level variables.

In Chapter 8, I develop and estimate a series of individual (district) level empirical models to predict the probability that an experienced challenger emerges to contest an incumbent in a U.S. House race using a set of independent variables. I estimate both overall models and separate models by party. In the overall model, I find incumbent spending in the previous election to be unrelated to the probability of a high-quality challenger. Greater challenger spending in the previous election cycle boosts the probability of an experienced challenger in the subsequent election, controlling for challenger performance in the previous election and lagged incumbent spending. I demonstrate that higher levels of incumbent party strength in the district, as evidenced in support for the incumbent party's presidential candidate in the previous election, and majority status in the U.S. House depress the likelihood of a quality challenger, and I show that state legislative term limits do not exert an effect on quality. For the most part, these findings remain consistent when the analyses are conducted by party, with one exception. I find the impact of majority status to boost the probability of an experienced Democratic challenger but to depress the likelihood of a quality Republican challenger. Using data from the 1974–2012 elections, for which data was available, I estimate a series of models to predict the probability of an experienced challenger adding the two additional state-level variables described in Chapter 7: State legislative professionalism and state-level party competition. I find that, unlike in Chapter 7, on average states with greater state legislative professionalism have a smaller proportion of quality challengers. When I estimate the model by party, I find consistent results for the effect of each of the variables except incumbent spending. I discuss the results in greater detail and make comparisons to the findings of the more aggregated analyses presented in Chapters 6 and Seven.

Based on the results of the analyses I conduct in Chapter 8, I present and discuss my conclusions about why I find challenger quality to be on the decline. I compute quantities of interest to offer meaningful conclusions about why experienced challengers appear less frequently to contest incumbents. I find no evidence that rising campaign costs account for the decline in quality over the period of this study. I do find support for the hypothesis that declining competitiveness helps to explain the decline in quality. The results presented in Chapter 8 show that declining competitiveness explains virtually all of the overall decline in quality.

In Chapter 9, I consider the implications of the findings reported in this study on American democracy by focusing on how the developments I observe are connected to incumbency advantage in elections. Overall, and by way of preview, I find that the incumbency advantage has declined over the period of this study, despite declining challenger quality in congressional elections. I reflect on the normative implications of these results for democratic responsiveness in America and conclude we may be wise to remain vigilant about the potential consequences of quality decline in U.S. elections.

Chapter 10 summarizes the main conclusions of this book and offers some additional concluding remarks.

Introduction

In Arizona's 1st congressional district, voters in the general election on November 2, 2004, had to decide whether or not to unseat incumbent Republican Rick Renzi. Renzi, a freshman lawmaker who was elected over disorganized Democratic opposition in 2002 with 49% of the vote, fought to hold his seat against Democrat Paul Babbitt, the brother of Bruce Babbitt—Arizona's former governor and secretary of the interior in the Clinton administration. Babbitt, a businessman, had been previously elected Mayor of Flagstaff and had served on the Flagstaff City Council. He was also elected and had served as Coconino County supervisor since 1986. Babbitt boasted that he had never lost an election. With incumbent Renzi facing a strong opponent with a demonstrated history of electoral viability, experts considered the race to be a toss-up despite the fact that Renzi ultimately won reelection.

By and large, congressional races like Arizona's 1st district in 2004 are rare. Incumbents are routinely perceived to be invulnerable in contemporary congressional elections, and they are challenged mainly by political neophytes who typically lack electoral experience and prior success at the polls. Consider that in the 2004 cycle, Bobby Rush, the 58-year-old incumbent Democrat in Illinois's 1st congressional district, faced opposition from Republican Raymond Wardingley, a 69-year-old local comedian with only a high school diploma and no prior elective experience. In California's 5th congressional district, veteran Democratic lawmaker Robert Matsui ran against Republican Mike Dugas, a 27-year-old doctoral student who had never run for office before. Republican George Radanovich, serving his fourth term representing California's 19th congressional district, faced James Bufford, a 52-year-old Democrat who owned the Strawberry Alarm Clock Company. Bufford was also pursuing his Bachelor's degree in Anthropology and had no prior elective experience. In Florida's 1st congressional district, Jeff Miller, the Republican incumbent who also served in the Florida State House between

6 Dynamics of Challenger Quality

1998 and 2001, faced opposition from Democrat Mark Coutu, a cook with no prior elective experience.

For the most part, such races have been the norm in congressional contests across the nation for at least the past four decades. Contests against incumbents rarely include challengers with prior elective political experience, or, as the political science literature characterizes them, "high-quality challengers." While many challengers are competent and committed to public service, they oftentimes lack the experience crucial to defeating an incumbent. As Sandy Maisel has put it,

> [w]hile the [electorally inexperienced candidate] may be well-liked and respected in their community, the average bank teller, contractor, grocer, or accountant is unlikely to mount a credible challenge to a House incumbent because they are not well-known and because, in all likelihood, they have not developed the political capital necessary to run a viable campaign.
>
> *(Maisel et al. 2001: 14).*

Examining the backgrounds of congressional candidates may yield useful insights about contemporary campaigns and elections, including the decline in electoral competition documented by many scholars (Maisel et al. 2001; Herrnson 1995; Ferejohn 1977) and incumbent reelection rates that have soared above 90% consistently over the past 21 election cycles, with the minor exception of 2010 (see Figure 1.1) (see also Jacobson 2000).

U.S. House incumbents who face no serious challenge cannot be removed from office. Their constituents have no direct electoral means of expressing

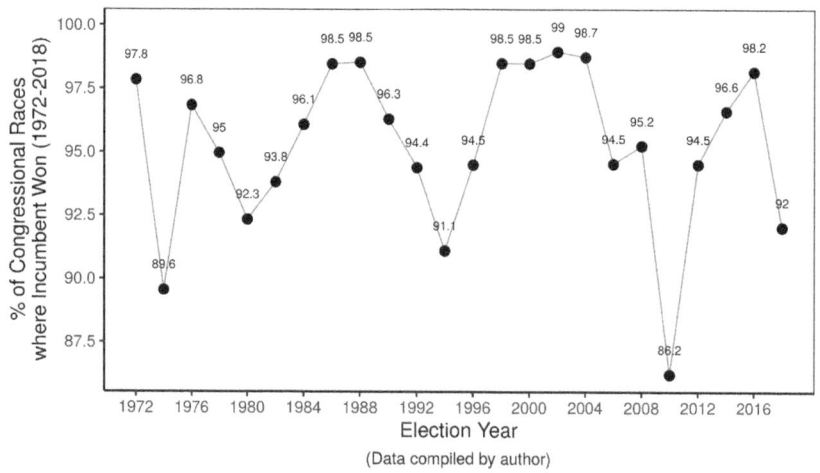

FIGURE 1.1 Reelection Rates for Incumbents, U.S. House (1972–2018)

dissatisfaction with their performance in office. Indeed, without a vigorous campaign mounted by a skilled opponent, many constituents lack the information necessary to assess their representative's performance and come to a reasoned judgment about whether the incumbent should continue in office. "[The] lack of meaningful contests in many House districts is a very troublesome aspect of contemporary American politics" (Maisel et al. 2001: 13).

Who are these "skilled opponents" that Maisel and his colleagues describe? Political scientists have long debated the definition of a "high-quality" challenger (see Chapter 2). There appears to be a general consensus in the literature, however, that candidates can be distinguished from each other based on a variety of characteristics in such a way that makes some more "skilled" (i.e., "high-quality") than others (i.e., "low-quality") and that high-quality challengers possess abilities and resources that enable them to launch more competitive campaigns against incumbents.

What Is "Challenger Quality"?

The notion of challenger quality was introduced by Gary Jacobson in 1978 (Jacobson 1978). Simply put, challenger quality is the experience challengers bring with them to a race. It exists prior to the campaign (Krasno 1994). Jacobson offers the most simple, dichotomous conceptualization: Challengers with prior successful electoral experience (those who have previously held elective office) are high-quality, while all others are low-quality.[1]

Since Jacobson initially conceptualized quality, scholars have argued for more refined measures of quality. Some researchers advocate alternative definitions of challenger quality (Bond, Fleisher, and Covington 1985; Krasno and Green 1988; Arnold and Hawkins 2002), while others focus on what conditions are likely to produce high-quality challengers (Jacobson 1989; Jacobson and Kernell 1981; Canon 1990; Banks and Kiewiet 1989) and on what the impact of challenger quality is on election outcomes (Krasno 1994; Jacobson 1992). Amidst the debate in the literature, an agreement seems to have emerged around two general points: That some challengers are better than others, and that this matters for elections.

Survey data suggests that the public prefers politically experienced candidates for Congress to inexperienced candidates. In a survey[2] conducted in May 1996 by NBC News and the *Wall Street Journal*, 31% of respondents indicated they would be "more likely" to vote for a candidate with no previous political experience compared with 47% who indicated they would be "less likely" to support a candidate with no political experience. (16% indicated that prior political experience does not make much difference, and 6% were not sure.) Unfortunately, this survey item was never repeated and no similar items have probed public attitudes about political experience and electoral support, so no comparative opinion data is available.

8 Dynamics of Challenger Quality

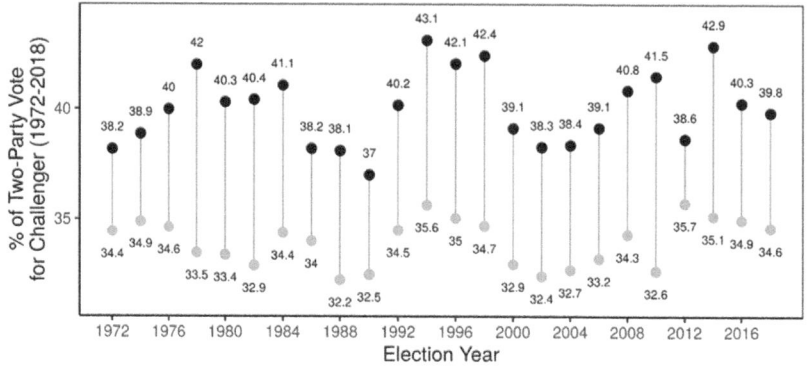

FIGURE 1.2 Average Challenger Voteshares by Experience (1972–2018)

Voters clearly indicate these preferences, however, through election returns. Besides the public's strong support for incumbents discussed above, politically experienced challengers fare better at the polls than political neophytes. Data presented in Figure 1.2 demonstrates that experienced challengers consistently outperform their inexperienced counterparts at the polls between 1972 and 2018. On average, experienced challengers' share of the two-party vote in contested elections over this period is about 6 percentage points higher than inexperienced challengers' average voteshare. These high-quality challengers do better than low-quality challengers at the polls, and an analysis of the data reveals a statistically significant difference ($p < 0.001$) in the electoral performance of these challengers attributable to experience during this period.

Jacobson (1990) also observes that experienced candidates are more likely to defeat incumbents. He estimates that experienced challengers are four times as likely as inexperienced challengers to defeat incumbents (Jacobson 1990). "Other things being equal, the strongest congressional candidates are those for whom politics is a career" (Jacobson and Carson 2016: 55). Jacobson shows similar results for open seat races. In (new) open seats held by neither party, experienced candidates win four of five contests against candidates who have never held elective office (Jacobson 1990).

Some work has attempted to delineate the forces that may affect the quality advantage. Buttice and Stone (2012) find that ideological polarization may diminish the effect of quality advantage (Buttice and Stone 2012). These works agree, however, that voters consistently prefer high-quality challengers over those with no prior elective experience, on average.

Jacobson also argues that the difference challenger quality makes in election outcomes grew between 1946 and 1988. He found that the growth in payoff for quality in terms of votes increased markedly, from 1.2 percentage points in 1946 to 4.3 percentage points in 1988 (Jacobson 1990: 56). Thus, the quality of a challenger not only matters, but it appears to matter increasingly more in election outcomes.

Challenger Quality Over Time

Despite a rich literature on candidate quality and—more broadly—on candidacy and candidate emergence, few analyses track developments over time in contemporary elections. Notably, Carson and Roberts (2014) conduct a fascinating study that examines quality dynamics in the era of party dominance using data on late 19th- and early 20th-century congressional races, but contemporary factors are not studied. In arguing for a comprehensive theory of candidacy, Linda Fowler (1993) posits that, among other things, such a theory should be, "dynamic to allow for changing expectations and circumstances that move politicians in and out of the candidate pool" (42). In her review and evaluation of the literature on candidate emergence and challenger quality, Fowler laments that "[t]he rational actor paradigm gives us a static view of the decision to run for Congress. The way the equation is set up, it provides a snapshot of the prospective office seeker's utility calculus at a particular moment. It lacks any provision for predicting how the individual calculus of office seeking has changed over time. Moreover, it leaves out the systemic effects of social and economic transformations that can affect the aggregate choices of candidates. In this respect, the rational actor approach to candidacy fails to account for long-term trends associated with eligibility, motivation, elite influence, and institutional structures" (64). "There are sound reasons," Fowler continues, "for presuming that ambition varies with the social and political environment and the individual's relation to that environment" (65).

Fowler's basic assertion is that, while there exists a vast literature on candidacy and candidate quality, the lack of scholarly emphasis on developments or temporal contextual changes in this area of inquiry limit the conclusions we can draw from existing work. Research that will, "move us closer to the integration of diverse intellectual traditions that the theoretical literature on candidates comprises … [should consider] how the supply of candidates for Congress adapts over time to broad social and institutional changes" (70).

Fowler repeatedly calls for closer attention to developments in aggregate levels of candidate quality over time. "Even as scholars employ more sophisticated methods to unravel what is cause and what is effect, they will need to address at least three other pressing methodological questions: the definition of candidate quality, the specification of local contexts, and the control for *changes across time*" [emphasis added] (112). Fowler observes that "[a] great deal of the existing research on congressional candidates relies on cross-sectional data. Most of the time series analysis has been conducted by scholars working on the question of strategic politicians and to a lesser extent by those studying campaign finance.

But the investigation of many important aspects of candidate emergence has been limited to a single year or a few years at most, even though the political environment in which candidates make their decisions to run for Congress has radically changed over the postwar period" (116).

Fowler's calls for additional research focusing on changes over time spawned few such studies in the decades that followed. While scholars turned their attention to important aspects of candidate emergence (for instance, Maisel and others' (2001) work on identifying and surveying potential candidates), little attention was directed to analyses across time. It is the primary aim of this book to explore the impact of developments in political and social context over the past four decades or so on changes in candidate quality in congressional elections.

Trends in Candidate Quality

The purpose of this book is to analyze trends in the quality of challengers that have emerged to contest incumbents between 1972 and 2018. In the first part of the book, I examine *aggregate patterns* for trends in candidate emergence that may help us better understand developments in contemporary congressional elections. The primary focus will be on races against incumbents for the U.S. House; however, I will also consider developments in U.S. Senate races and open seat races for the U.S. House to illustrate some points. This book updates, expands, and is guided by work pioneered by Jacobson (1990), Canon (1990), and Carson and Roberts (2014).

Rational Choice, Ambition Theory, and Challenger Quality

Researchers interested in politicians' career paths are often guided by ambition theory, initially developed and applied to electoral politics by Schlesinger (1966). Schlesinger believes that, "[a]mbition lies at the heart of politics, and that politics thrive on the hope of preferment and the drive for office" (1966:1). Broadly conceptualized, ambition theory posits that politicians' actions are fueled by their prospective political ambition. Schlesinger distinguishes between three forms of ambition: *discrete* (those who aim to attain a specific office for a limited, temporary period), *static* (those who aim to attain a specific office for the long term), and *progressive* (those who constantly seek upward moves to higher elective positions) (Schlesinger 1966; Farmer et al. 2003).

Subsequent research refines Schlesinger's notion of ambition theory. Black (1972) and Rhode (1979) modify the theory to cast it in utility maximizing form (Aldrich 1995). In these reformulations, which represent a partial departure from Schlesinger's original argument, all incumbents are assumed to prefer holding a higher office to a lower office and all prefer holding office to holding no office at all (Aldrich 1995). If politicians are careerists and if higher office is so desirable, ambition theory implies that there will generally be more aspirants than available offices (Aldrich 1995: 22). *We may reasonably infer, thus, that higher-level offices will be contested—almost always—by incumbents who hold lower level seats.* Such candidates would be—by the Jacobson definition—high-quality challengers.

But this reasoning may be oversimplified. The actions of rational actors are determined by cost-benefit calculations that must take into consideration not only the costs of an action but also the benefit discounted by the likelihood of attaining the benefit. Rational actors will only act if the benefit, discounted by the probability of attaining it, outweighs the cost of attainment. These calculations affect the decisions of potential candidates in seeking office. Formalizing and extending the argument, Rhode (1979) uses the example of an incumbent House member who is deciding between running for reelection, running for the U.S. Senate, or retiring. The three possible outcomes are:

1. Holding no office $\{O_n\}$,
2. Keeping their current House seat $\{O_h\}$,
3. Winning a Senate seat $\{O_s\}$.

Ambition theory assumes that:

$$U(O_s) > U(O_h) > U(O_n) \text{ or, effectively, } U(O_n) = 0.$$

The set of action choices for the incumbent is:

1. Run for no office $\{a_n\}$,
2. Run for reelection $\{a_h\}$,
3. Run for Senate $\{a_s\}$.

Each action is costly, and, presumably, running for higher office (Senate) is more costly. Costs may be characterized as:

$$C_s > C_h > C_n = 0.$$

Utility maximization (assuming $U(O_n) = 0$) makes the action choice dependent on two probabilities: The probability of election to the Senate (House) if the incumbent runs and the respective probabilities of defeat. (Summarized in Aldrich 1995: 51. See Rhode (1979) for details.) In the end, the rational incumbent will retire if the costs of running for either office outweigh the expected benefits. If not, the candidate opts to run for the office that offers the higher net benefit. For the incumbent House member, the probability of reelection is so high (positive) that retirement is unusual. The probability of winning a Senate seat is lower, with higher costs. Aldrich (1995: 52) explains that candidates must either be very ambitious or time a Senate race carefully (at a point when the probability of winning the Senate seat is especially high) in order to seek the Senate seat over reelection.

For the individual incumbent House member, there are few incentives to run for higher office. More generally, incumbents, who would be high-quality challengers, are unlikely to risk losing their current seat to run for higher office. *The expectation that emerges from this work, therefore, is that few high-quality challengers will seek to unseat incumbents.*

"Strategic Politicians" and Challenger Quality

Extant literature suggests that strong challengers do not emerge randomly. The most developed theoretical argument—the "strategic politicians thesis" proposed by Jacobson and Kernell—suggests that the occurrence of high-quality challengers varies with the prospects of victory (Jacobson 1989). Politicians—behaving as rational actors—will be "strategic" in their decision to run against incumbents and will opt to challenge incumbents when conditions make incumbents most vulnerable (Jacobson and Kernell 1981; Jacobson 1989; Maisel et al. 2001). By and large, high-quality challengers prefer to wait for an open seat in which there is no incumbent with their requisite advantages (Jacobson and Kernell 1981; Banks and Kiewiet 1989; Cox and Katz 2002; Carson and Roberts 2014). But potential challengers take many circumstances into consideration when attempting to determine the incumbent's degree of vulnerability, both national conditions and district-level conditions (Jacobson 1989; Jacobson and Kernell 1981). Local conditions include the percentage of votes previously won by the candidate of the challenger's party, and whether or not the seat switched party hands in the previous election; national conditions include the economy and presidential approval (typically, a "party of administration" variable added in as a control) (Jacobson 1989). Together these local and national conditions will determine the probability that a high-quality challenger will oppose the incumbent. There is evidence that experienced challengers have become more selective over time. Since 2000, over 40% of quality candidates have run in congressional districts with favorable conditions, compared to 25% in the period between 1946 and 2000 (Jacobson and Carson 2015).

Some literature does exist that finds alternate motivations for candidate emergence. Carson (2005) finds that experienced challengers are more likely to emerge if the incumbent has been increasingly voting with their party on prominent roll calls. In related work, Carson et al. (2011) find that state legislators are much more likely to enter primaries if there is congruence between their state legislative districts and the congressional districts (Carson et al. 2011). Despite this work, the strategic voter theory delineated by Jacobson (1989) remains the academic standard for understanding the strategy behind challenging incumbents.

Thus, potential challengers' decisions to run against incumbents will depend greatly on the probability of achieving the benefits associated with being elected and the costs of running. National and local conditions affect these factors and will advantage potential challengers of one party during certain election cycles and disadvantage potential challengers of the other party in those races. Consequently, high-quality challengers of one party will emerge when conditions favor them and make the incumbent (of the opposing party) vulnerable. Studies of individual-level strategic behavior confirm this proposition (Jacobson and Kernell 1981; Jacobson 1989; Bond, Covington, and Fleisher 1985). Generally speaking, when conditions favor Democrats, the Democratic party is more successful in recruiting a greater proportion of higher-quality challengers against Republican incumbents. Conversely, when conditions favor Republicans, the Republican party is more successful at recruiting a greater proportion of high-quality challengers to Democratic incumbents (Jacobson and Kernell 1981). Jacobson (2015) finds an increase in this pattern in 21st-century elections. He posits that contemporary strategic challengers take into account nonpartisan conditions less and instead decide to "ride the electoral tide" more (Jacobson 2015). Jacobson and Kernell (1981) also suggest that high-quality challengers, often incumbents with a great deal more to lose than inexperienced amateurs, are more "strategic" than low-quality challengers (see also Jacobson 1990).

Several reasonable expectations emerge from the strategic politicians theory. Previous studies make clear why it may be reasonable to observe variation over time between the two parties' proportion of high-quality challengers against incumbents. Some cycles will be strong for Democrats and others for Republicans. In the aggregate, however, over time, as these party-specific and cycle-specific differences cancel out, we should observe an equilibrium level of challenger quality for all candidates. It is reasonable to conclude that as the variation cancels out, *the proportion of high-quality challengers of both parties in the aggregate over time should be systematically flat*. Indeed, previous research has revealed few trends in aggregate levels of challenger quality over time (Jacobson 1990; Lublin 1994). I investigate whether or not this remains true for the period of interest by replicating some of Jacobson's basic analyses.

A second extension of the strategic politician thesis also arises in this analysis. As potential candidates increasingly have access to data and information that enables them to be strategic (Fowler 1993), we would expect that, even if fewer high-quality challengers face off against incumbents when conditions are not ripe, open seat contests that do not include an incumbent should attract *more* high-quality candidates than races against incumbents. Researchers have demonstrated this to be the case (Canon 1990; Jacobson 1990; Gaddie and Bullock 2000). I will also investigate whether or not this remains the case during the period of interest. We may also hypothesize, however, that *open seats should be attracting increasingly greater proportions of high-quality candidates over time*.

Finding Trends

To conduct these initial analyses, I examine data on challenger quality in contested elections for the U.S. House of Representatives in which an incumbent was running for reelection between 1972 and 2018. This period was not selected arbitrarily. In the analyses that follow, I will rely partly on campaign expenditure data to explain the phenomenon we observe. For all intents and purposes, reliable campaign expenditure data is only available post-1972. My empirical analyses are computed using a comprehensive district-level dataset of 16,098 observations total, aggregated variously and as indicated across the analyses.

For current purposes, I define *challenger quality* as a dichotomous variable that incorporates only whether or not challengers have had previous political experience as elected officials (Jacobson and Kernell 1981). Earlier I discussed that several scholars have argued that measures of challenger quality that are less crude would be more accurate (Bond, Covington, and Fleisher 1985; Krasno and Green 1988; Arnold and Hawkins 2002). They contend that conceptualizing candidate quality solely as a function of previous political experience as elected officials is faulty and argue that Jacobson and Kernell's dichotomous variable disregards other important indicators of quality such as professional and/or celebrity status (Arnold and Hawkins 2002) Despite these refinements, Jacobson and Kernell's original formulation retains strong explanatory power and is commonly adopted in the literature (Cox and Katz 2002; Carson and Roberts 2014).

Aggregating to the national level for each congressional cycle between 1972 and 2018, I have determined the *aggregate proportion of incumbents facing high-quality challengers* for each election cycle. I also compute these proportions by party.

In analyzing similar data over an earlier—and longer—postwar period (1946–1988), Jacobson (1990) observed few discernible trends in the overall level of challenger quality. Figure 1.3 shows that the aggregate proportion of high-quality

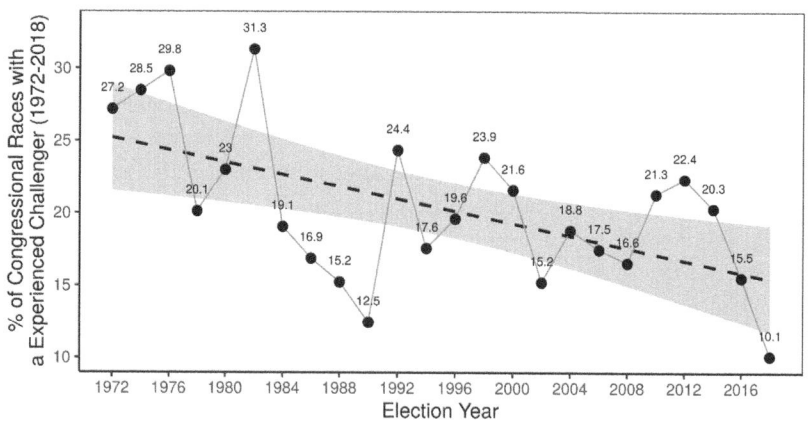

(Data compiled by author from Jacobson Challenger Quality Measures)
Note: The dashed line and 95% confidence interval gives the OLS regression line determined by the data.)

FIGURE 1.3 Proportion of Incumbents Facing Experienced Challengers, U.S. House, (1972–2018)

challengers has varied greatly between 1972 and 2018, ranging from 10 to 31% of all challengers. Despite this variation, the aggregate proportion of high-quality challengers has never exceeded a 31% peak in 1982. In fact, in the average election cycle, only 20.3% of incumbents face high-quality challengers.

More importantly, analysis of the data reported in Figure 1.3 reveals that the overall proportion of high-quality challengers in the aggregate has systematically *declined* between 1972 and 2018. A simple OLS regression[3] shows that, in the aggregate, the proportion of high-quality challengers has decreased significantly, by approximately 0.4 percentage points (standard error = 0.13) each election cycle (N = 24. p < .01 level). Substantively, this implies that the U.S. electorate—as a whole—has had fewer and fewer high-quality challengers to choose from in U.S. House races across the country since 1972.

The findings reveal that the overall aggregate level of challenger quality in U.S. House races has declined in the U.S. during this period. Can we glean insights about this decline by examining aggregate challenger quality levels by party during this period? Figure 1.4 presents data on the dynamics of challenger quality by party between 1972 and 2018. The analysis shows variation in aggregate levels of challenger quality by party during this period. We observe that the Democratic party has generally yielded a greater share of high-quality challengers than the Republican party; on average, 23% of Democratic challengers have been high-quality during this period compared with 18% of Republican challengers.

An analysis of the data presented in Figure 1.4 reveals that both parties have experienced statistically significant declines in aggregate challenger quality during this period, but some compelling partisan differences also emerge. The decline

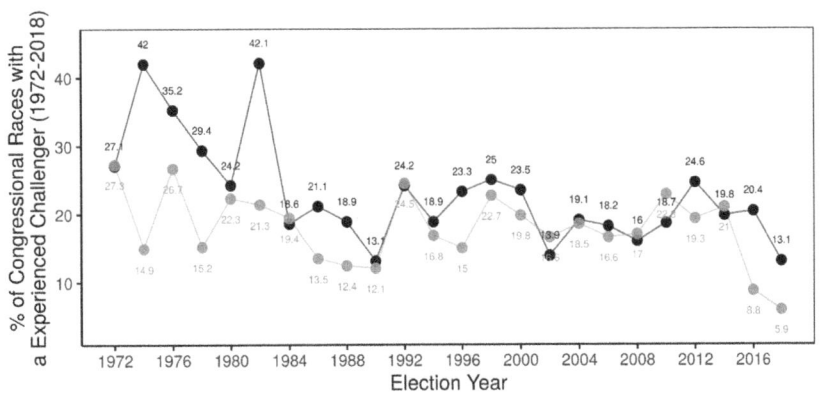

FIGURE 1.4 Proportion of Experienced Challengers by Party, U.S. House (1972–2018)

has been somewhat more acute for Democrats. While the share of experienced, Republican challengers has declined by about 0.3 percentage points per cycle on average (OLS regression coefficient -0.28, $t = -1.85$), average elective experience has dropped by more than twice this rate for Democratic challengers (OLS time series regression coefficient $= -0.68$, $t = -3.69$).

In the 1970s and 1980s, Jacobson (1990: 63) observed that the Republican party was finding it increasingly difficult to recruit experienced challengers. Indeed, Jacobson (1990) believed this deficiency to be partly accountable for the Democratic dominance of Congress in the postwar era. By the 1990s, however, Republicans exhibited greater strength in recruiting experienced challengers, even as Democratic success in recruiting high-quality hopefuls dwindled.[4]

U.S. Senate

By way of comparison, let us consider briefly developments in contested elections for the U.S. Senate. U.S. Senate elections differ from U.S. House elections in important ways (Abramowitz 1984; Abramowitz and Segal 1992; Krasno 1994). In particular, Senate incumbents have markedly lower reelection rates compared to House incumbents. Scholars have considered a variety of factors to explain this gap, but the most widely held view is that Senate incumbents are less successful than their counterparts in the House because Senate challengers are better than House challengers (Jacobson 2000; Krasno 1994; Squire 1992; Lublin 1994). The prevailing election's nostrum that "you can't beat somebody with nobody" seems to hold. "Senators lose more often because they are more likely to face formidable challengers who manage to wage intense campaigns. Based on their previous experiences, Senate challengers are usually better candidates—combining attractiveness and political skill—than the people who run against House incumbents" (Krasno 1994: 154). Put differently, the average Senate challenger is "higher quality" than the average House challenger.

Empirical analyses confirm this assertion. Krasno reports that, based on his measure of quality (Krasno 1994; Krasno and Green 1988; see below), the average Senate challenger has more than four times the political quality of the average House challenger. The Senate may attract more experienced challengers in part because the term is longer, or because it is a higher profile, more attractive institution (Baker 1995).

This section will examine the dynamics of challenger quality in elections for the U.S. Senate between 1972 and 2012.[5] I will present empirical findings about trends in challenger quality over time. I have determined the *proportion of Senate incumbents facing high-quality challengers* in the aggregate for each election cycle. The analysis confirms that overall Senate challenger quality exceeds House challenger quality consistently throughout this period. It also reveals that challenger quality in Senate elections has varied over time but that, although there has been a *decline* in aggregate challenger quality during this period, it is not statistically significant.

Dynamics of Challenger Quality   17

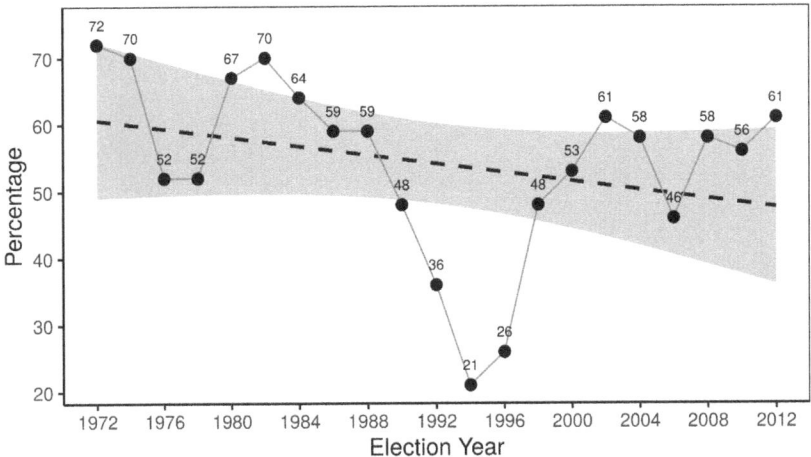

FIGURE 1.5 Proportion of Experienced Challengers, U.S. Senate Elections (1972–2012)

Figure 1.5 shows that the aggregate proportion of high-quality challengers has varied greatly between 1972 and 2012, ranging from 21 to 72% of all Senate challengers. Despite this variation, the aggregate proportion of high-quality challengers has never exceeded a 72% peak in 1972. In fact, in the average election cycle, only slightly more than half (54%) of U.S. Senate incumbents seeking reelection face high-quality challengers.

Analysis of the data reported in Figure 1.5 reveals that the overall proportion of high-quality challengers in the aggregate has *declined* between 1972 and 2012, although this decline is not statistically significant. A simple OLS regression shows that, in the aggregate, the proportion of high-quality challengers has decreased by 0.6 percentage points on average for each election cycle (standard error = 0.48; N = 21. Adjusted R-squared = 0.04; t = − 1.36).

The analysis still suggests that the U.S. electorate—as a whole—has had fewer high-quality challengers—more "nobodies"—to choose from in U.S. Senate races across the country since 1972. Figure 1.6 demonstrates that overall Senate challenger quality levels remain higher than overall House quality levels during this period. In fact, on average, Senators seeking reelection are more than twice as likely to face high-quality challengers than House incumbents (54% versus 21%, respectively). The analysis of the data also reveals that Senate challenger quality is declining slightly faster than aggregate House challenger quality, although only the decline in House challenger quality is statistically significant. (The rate of decline in aggregate House challenger quality over this period was 0.4 percentage points per cycle; see above.)

18 Dynamics of Challenger Quality

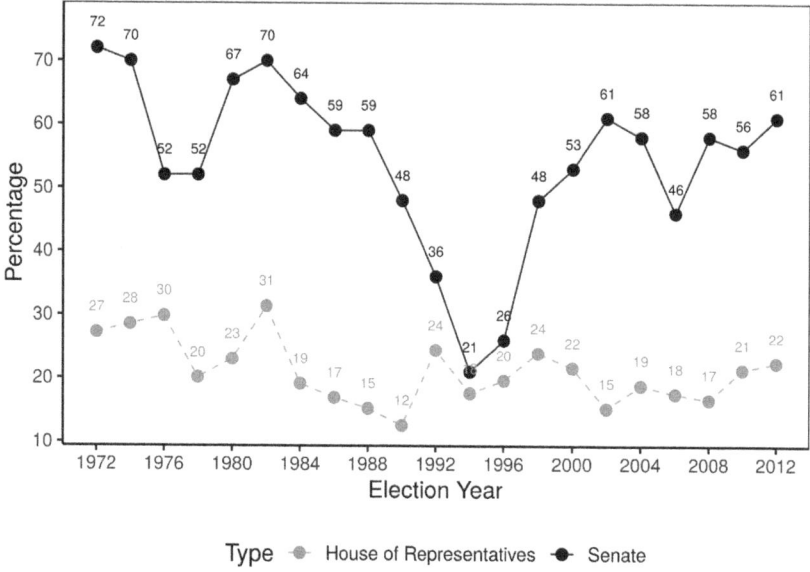

FIGURE 1.6 Proportion of Experienced Challengers, House and Senate (1972–2012)

Open Seats

Jacobson and Kernell's (1981) strategic politicians theory asserts that potential candidates will evaluate the political climate when making the decision to run against an incumbent. This means that they will most likely opt to enter races against incumbents when the conditions are most unfavorable for incumbents. Strategic politicians will consider both national and district-level factors during the decision-making process and are more likely than inexperienced candidates to wait for a seat to become vacant before tossing their hat into the electoral ring. Kazee (1994) finds that most potential challengers, particularly experienced hopefuls, are risk averse. Given the weak odds of unseating an incumbent, Kazee argues that it may be rational to forego a congressional challenge. A failed challenge can wound political prospects, saddle a loser with debt, surround him or her by the "stench of defeat," and may often require the challenger to pass up reelection (Gaddie and Bullock 2000). In this regard, experienced politicians, for whom the stakes are highest, will presumably be more "strategic" than inexperienced, low-quality potential candidates who have less to lose by entering even hopeless races against incumbents. These more strategic politicians "await a propitious moment before attempting to move up the office-holding ladder," (Gaddie and Bullock 2000: 7) oftentimes waiting for open seats.

Open seats, then, should attract greater percentages of high-quality candidates than do contests against incumbents. Studies reveal this to be the case (Jacobson 1980; Gaddie and Bullock 2000; Canon 1990; Cox and Katz 2002). Experienced candidates are more common in open seat races than in contests against challengers. The data presented in Figures 1.7, 1.8, and 1.9 reveal similar

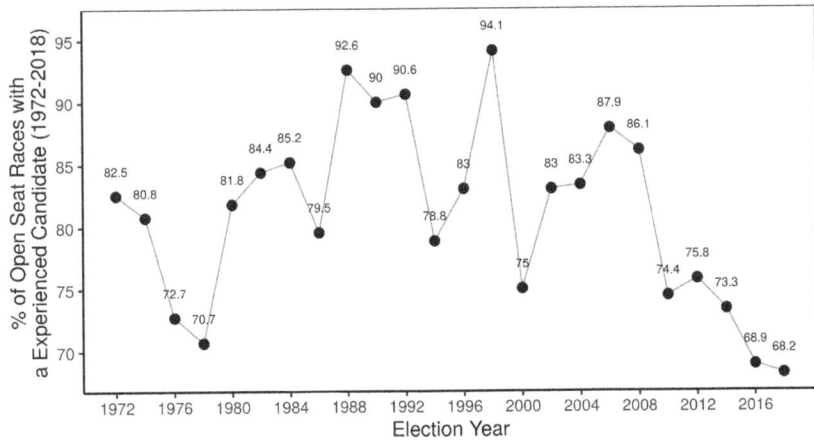

FIGURE 1.7 Proportion of Open Seat HR Races with at Least One Experienced Candidate (General Election) (1972–2018)

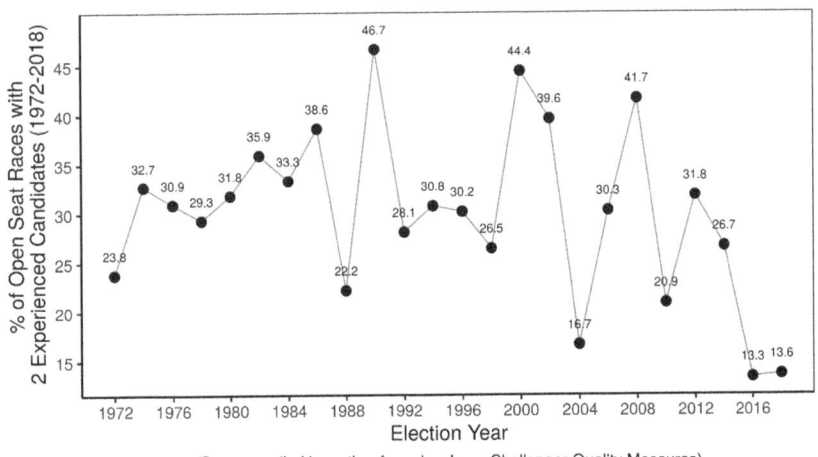

FIGURE 1.8 Proportion of Open Seat HR Races with Two Experienced Candidates (General Election) (1972–2018)

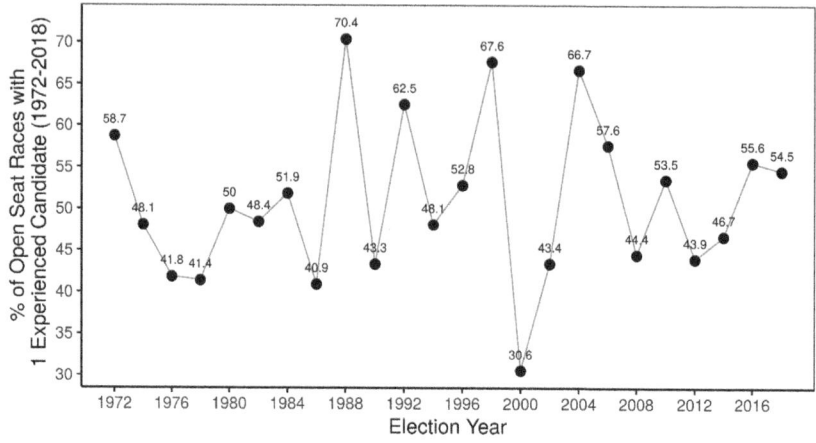

FIGURE 1.9 Proportion of Open Seat HR Races with One Experienced Candidate (General Election) (1972–2018)

findings for the period 1972–2018. On average, half (51%) of open seats during this period have attracted one experienced candidate in the general election (versus only 20% of contests against incumbents during the same period; see above) and 30% of open seat contests, on average, have attracted two high-quality candidates.

One plausible explanation, thus, for the decline in aggregate levels of high-quality challengers in races for the U.S. House is that experienced candidates are increasingly "more strategic," in their calculations. In the end, more and more high-quality candidates wait for open seat races rather than challenging incumbents. *We may hypothesize, thus, that the overall aggregate proportion of high-quality candidates in open seat races for the U.S. House should have increased systematically.* Put another way, potential candidates, especially experienced politicians, are increasingly "more strategic" in their career choices.

Jacobson (1980) observes that competition for open seats increased between 1946 and 1988. In his 1981 study, Jacobson expects—and finds—increasing concentration of high-quality candidates in contests for open seats. His findings reveal increases in the aggregate proportion of experienced open seat candidates for both the party currently holding the seat and the out-party (Jacobson 1980: 66).

The time series data presented in Figures 1.7–1.9, however, tell a different story. The anticipated increase in the aggregate proportions of high-quality candidates in open seat races for the U.S. House is not supported by the findings. Figure 1.9 shows that the proportion of open seat races between 1972–2018 that have attracted one high-quality candidate has ranged between 31% and 70%, but a simple, OLS regression reveals no traceable trend over time (Coefficient = 0.11; S.E. = 0.29; $p < 0.70$; N = 24). Similarly, we observe no significant increase in the aggregate proportion of open seat races that have attracted two high-quality candidates during the same period (OLS: Coefficient = 0.39; S.E. 0.25; $p < 0.14$; N = 24) (Data presented in Figure 1.7).

Jacobson also finds notable differences by party in the incidence of high-quality candidates in open seat contests for the U.S. House. His data for the 1946–1988 period demonstrate that, while there was increased concentration of experienced candidates for open seat races for both parties, Republicans are more likely than Democrats to field high-quality candidates when they are the incumbent party, while Democrats are more likely than Republicans to field experienced candidates when the other party holds the seat (Jacobson 1980: 67).

The data presented in Figure 1.10 suggest that overall, between 1972 and 2018, the Democratic party fielded a slightly higher proportion of high-quality candidates than the Republican party for open seat contests early on. On average, Democrats fielded high-quality candidates in 57% of open seat races during this period, compared with 53% of races for the Republican party. More telling perhaps is that neither party fielded increasingly more experienced candidates for open seat races over this period. Simple OLS regressions reveal a modest, but significant decrease for Democrats (Coefficient = -0.58; S.E. = 0.26; $p < 0.05$; N = 24), and no significant change for Republicans (Coefficient = -0.08; S.E. = 0.28; $p < 0.77$; N = 24).

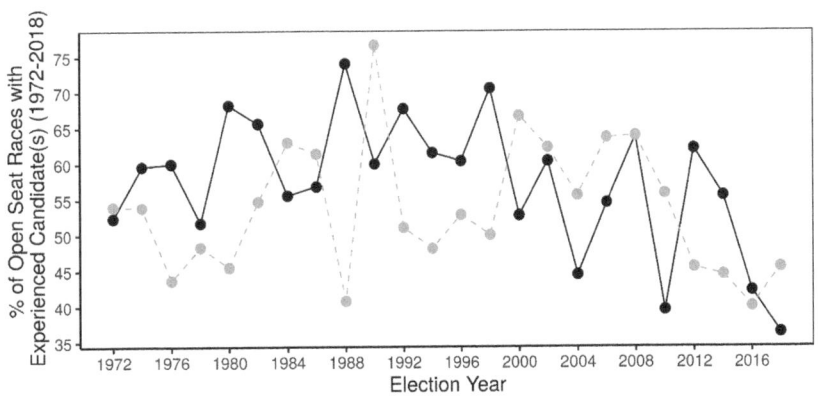

(Data compiled by author from Jacobson Challenger Quality Measures)

FIGURE 1.10 Proportion of Open Seat HR Races by Experienced Candidate, by Party (General Election) (1972–2018)

Redistricting: An Alternative Explanation for Declining Quality?

Recent scholarship (Cox and Katz 2002) finds that the increasing predictability and regularity of redistricting that followed the Supreme Court's 1966 *Wesberry v. Sanders* reapportionment decision causes strong contenders and incumbents to coordinate strategically in order to avoid facing off against each other in elections. The argument, described further in Chapters 2 and 3, suggests that quality challengers bide their time, waiting for election cycles that follow redistricting when their prospects for victory may be greater. Cox and Katz (2002) do find evidence of such an effect. Is it possible then, that the decline in overall challenger quality we observe between 1972 and 2018 is driven by developments in the redistricting process? Do quality challengers simply wait for redistricting, as some scholars argue they wait for open seat races, thereby artificially depressing overall proportion of quality challengers in election cycles that occur between redistrictings?

Below, I briefly consider the effect of redistricting on the aggregate proportions of challenger quality in election cycles. In the analyses I conduct in Chapter 8, which rely largely on the measurement of lagged values of the key variables in the district, I exclude redistricted districts. My analyses in Chapter 8, therefore, are silent about the effect of redistricting on the emergence of a quality challenger. The model specifications I advance, therefore, do not permit me to conclude that redistricting can help to explain the overall decline in challenger quality I observe over this period. Redistricting years represent only five cycles over the period of my analysis, however, 1972, 1982, 1992, 2002, and 2012 would have been excluded in the analyses that use lagged variables in my study. There were also districts whose boundaries were changed in 1974, 1984, 1986, 1994, 2003, and in other years, but these cases represent only a limited number of cases.

Moreover, several additional observations cause me to be skeptical about attributing the decline in challenger quality to redistricting. First, Cox and Katz (2002) essentially compare the pre-Wesberry period with the post-Wesberry period and observe a change (increase) in the presence of quality challengers as a result of redistricting. My analysis takes place entirely over the post-Wesberry period, so comparisons may not necessarily be parallel. I also find that the presence of an experienced challenger in races against incumbents in redistricted districts has not increased substantially over the period of my study. A district-level regression of the presence of a quality challenger on time and a constant reveals a statistically significant *decrease* when the analysis is limited to redistricted districts between 1972 and 2018 (coefficient $=-0.004$; standard error $=0.001$; $p < 0.01$; $N = 1,819$). Thus we see there was a decline of quality contenders in these districts, similar to the decline we observe more generally in congressional races during the same period. Even as the overall proportion of quality challengers in redistricted districts is slightly higher than non-redistricted races (23% to 20% respectively) over this period, I observe no general pattern of *increasing* presence of quality challengers after redistricting in this period. The overall proportion of high-quality challengers in 1972 is 20%. This proportion increases to 31% in 1982 but then drops to 24% in 1992. In 2002 the proportion of high-quality challengers decreased again to 15% before increasing to 22% in 2012. These observations suggest redistricting, as an alternative explanation for the decline in challenger quality, fails to account for the decline in challenger quality we observe in congressional elections between 1972 and 2018, at least given the limited number of observations of redistricting years. If redistricting is part of the picture, its effects likely manifest indirectly through changes reflected in the changing partisan composition of districts which influences competitiveness. I elaborate on the impact of competitiveness below and in the chapters that follow.

The Puzzle

The data presented in this analysis demonstrates that the overall aggregate level of challenger quality in races against incumbents has declined in congressional elections between 1972 and 2018. High-quality candidates may be "more strategic" than inexperienced candidates, but the analysis rejects the notion that experienced candidates are *increasingly* more strategic. *The aggregate decline in challenger quality does not coincide with a corresponding increase in the aggregate level of candidate quality in open seat races. Put simply, challenger quality has dropped between 1972 and 2018, but candidate quality in open seat races has not gone up.*

Now that we have documented the decline in candidate quality between 1972 and 2018, the findings leave us with a nontrivial puzzle: *Why are experienced candidates increasingly less likely to contest congressional races in the United States?* The remainder of this book aims to resolve this puzzle.

Notes

1 I use the terms "high-quality" and "experienced" interchangeably in this book. Candidates described as either high-quality or experienced simply have held prior elective office. All others are low-quality, or inexperienced.
2 (I'm going to mention several things you might learn about a candidate for Congress in your district. For each one, please tell me if this would make you more likely or less likely to vote for this candidate.) If a candidate … is not a politician and has no previous experience in government … would this make you more likely or less likely to support this candidate? (If "more likely", ask:) Would this make you much more likely or somewhat more likely to support this candidate? (If "less likely", ask:) Would this make you much less likely or somewhat less likely to support this candidate? Much more likely to support (11%); Somewhat more likely to support (20%); Somewhat less likely to support (24%); Much less likely to support (23%); Not make much difference (16%); Not sure (6%%). Survey by NBC News, Wall Street Journal. Methodology: Conducted by Hart and Teeter Research Companies, May 10–May 14, 1996, and based on telephone interviews with a national registered voters sample of 1,001.

3 Throughout this study, OLS time series coefficients indicate the estimated slope of the coefficient from a regression of the dependent variable on a constant and a time trend.
4 This phenomenon may account partly for the impressive Republican gains in Congress in 1994 and the party's sustained strength in the elections that followed.
5 Senate data only available through 2012.

2
CHALLENGER QUALITY— CONCEPTUALIZATION AND MEASUREMENT

> At present, candidate quality has the same status in the congressional literature that pornography enjoys in the opinions of the Supreme Court; that is to say, scholars recognize a quality candidate when they see one, but they disagree about just what individual attributes are most salient to the definition.
>
> *(Fowler 1993: 112)*

More than two decades later, Linda Fowler's apt characterization persists. Even as scholars have reached some consensus about the relevance of candidate quality in congressional elections, there exists ample methodological variation in the conceptualization and measurement of the variable in the scholarly literature.

Indeed, much of the controversy over candidate quality, and, in turn, challenger quality, is centered around definitions of the concept. In Jacobson's original (1978) formulation (and in most of his subsequent studies), only prior office-holding experience was the politically relevant criterion for designation as a high-quality candidate. Jacobson's dichotomous measure excludes considerations of *when* a candidate may have held office and does not distinguish between various levels of elective office. Presumably, this measurement encompasses a variety of dimensions and advantageous candidate characteristics: Political ambition, voter appeal, name recognition, organizational and coalition-building skills, and fundraising ability (Fowler 1993: 112). Politicians who have successfully attained elective office exhibit "prima facie evidence that the candidate has all or enough of the important attributes to win again" (Fowler 1993: 113). Squire (1995) posits, "previous political experience is a surrogate for the positive personal characteristics associated with higher quality challengers because we take it to be a concrete manifestation of them."

DOI: 10.4324/9781315164649-2

This simple dichotomous conceptualization is popular among many scholars who employ candidate quality as a variable in a variety of analyses. Bond, Fleisher and Talbert (1997), for example, espouse this measure in their analysis of open seat races for the U.S. House. Born (1986), Bianco (1984), Ragsdale and Cook (1987), Abramowitz (1988), Biersack, Herrnson, and Wilcox (1993), Van Dunk (1997), Cox and Katz (2002), Carson and Roberts (2014), Pyeatt (2014), Desmarais, La Raja, and Cowl (2014), Barnes, Branton, and Cassese (2017), Arceneaux et al. (2020), and Sparks (2020) also employ the binary measure in their work.

Disagreement about quality measurement surfaced quickly after the notion was introduced. Scholars argued for more refined measures of quality that were more sensitive to possible variation in political experience. After all, skills useful for running for dogcatcher are not necessarily relevant or sufficient in a campaign for Congress. "To ignore these differences," argues Fowler, as the original measure does, is to, "lump individuals of widely divergent political caliber in one category as 'quality' candidates and to relegate some very promising politicians to the residual category. Measurement error is the inevitable consequence" (Fowler 1993: 113).

Subsequent studies provide a variety of alternative formulations and measurements of quality. Table 2.1 summarizes the conceptualizations employed in notable studies. By and large, researchers rely on experience as the most salient component of candidate quality, but some offer more detailed differentiation of political experience.

Bond, Covington, and Fleisher (1985) are among the first scholars to recast the concept of quality in their study of challengers for the U.S. House in the 1980 elections. The authors view challenger quality as a function of both campaign finances (the natural log of challenger expenditures) and political experience (elective). Thus, they analyze both of these components as separate measures of quality as well as a composite measure that combines the two. Their measure of experience is a three-point ordinal scale: Challengers who were previously members of the state legislature, former members of Congress, or former candidates who had attained more than 40% of the vote in a previous congressional race, score three; challengers score two if they held an elected city or county office or if they had some other "politically useful" experience (congressional aide, member of a politically prominent family in the district, party official, etc.); all other challengers score one.

Other scholars offer additional refinements to the measure. Green and Krasno (1988) further expand the specification. The Green–Krasno index of quality incorporates professional, celebrity, and elective activities into one measure ranging from zero to eight. Candidates who had held elective office are coded four, and their score increases by +1 for: Incumbency in an elective office, holding high office, prior run for the House, and celebrity status. Candidates who have not held elective office start with a score of zero and increase by +1 for the following factors: Party activism, having run for office, having previously run for the

TABLE 2.1 Quality—Conceptualization and Measurement

Source	Seat Type	Quality Conceptualization
Jacobson (1978)	U.S. House	Dichotomous (1 = prior elective office; 0 = no prior elective office)
Bond, Covington, and Fleisher (1985)	U.S. House	Three-point, ordinal scale
Born (1986)	U.S. House	Dichotomous (1 = prior elective office; 0 = no prior elective office)
Krasno and Green (1988)	U.S. Senate	Nine-point scale (0–8)
Squire (1989)	U.S. Senate	Two ways: Seven-point ordinal scale (0–6); 300–500 point scale
Banks and Kiewiet (1989)	U.S. House	Three-point scale (strong/medium/weak)
Canon (1990)	U.S. House, U.S. Senate, Open Seats	Four-point scale (1–4)
Bond, Fleisher and Talbert (1997)	U.S. House, Open Seats	Dichotomous (1 = prior elective office; 0 = no prior elective office)
Krasno (1994)	U.S. House and U.S. Senate	Nine-point scale (0–8)
Lublin (1994)	U.S. Senate	Five-point scale (0–4)
Adams and Squire (1997)	U.S. Senate	0–600 point scale
Van Dunk (1997)	State Legislature	Dichotomous (1 = prior elective office; 0 = no prior elective office)
Gaddie and Bullock (2000)	Open Seats	Nine-point scale/Krasno and Green measure (open seats)
Gronke (2001)	U.S. House & U.S. Senate (combined)	Four-point scale (1–4)/Canon (1990) measure
Cox and Katz (2002)	U.S. House	Dichotomous (1 = prior elective office; 0 = no prior elective office)
Carson and Roberts (2005)	U.S. House and Senate	Dichotomous (1 = prior elective office; 0 = no prior elective office)
Carson, Engstrom, and Roberts (2007)	U.S. House	Dichotomous (1 = prior elective office; 0 = no prior elective office)
Buttice and Stone (2012)	U.S. House	Two measures: Difference in Experience (Rep. - Dem.) (5-point scale) Difference in Quality (Rep. – Dem.) on a 7-point scale
Carson and Roberts (2014)	U.S. House	Dichotomous (1 = prior elective office; 0 = no prior elective office)
Praino, Stockemer, and Moscardelli (2013)	U.S. House	3-point scale (1 = no prior elective office, 2 = prior elective office, 3 = Former US Rep.)

(Continued)

TABLE 2.1 (*Continued*)

Source	Seat Type	Quality Conceptualization
Pyeatt (2014)	U.S. House & Senate	Dichotomous (1 = prior elective office; 0 = no prior elective office)
Desmarais, La Raja, and Kowl (2014)	U.S. House	Dichotomous (1 = prior elective office; 0 = no prior elective office)
Barnes, Branton, and Cassese (2017)	U.S. House	Dichotomous (1 = prior elective office; 0 = no prior elective office)
Arceneaux, Dunaway, Johnson, and Vander Wielen (2019)	U.S. House	Dichotomous (1 = prior elective office; 0 = no prior elective office)
Sparks (2020)	U.S. House (California/ Washington)	Dichotomous (1 = prior elective office; 0 = no prior elective office)

Source: Compiled by Author.

U.S. House, professional status (lawyer, professor, or other profession that involves public speaking), appointive office, or celebrity status (Green and Krasno 1988; Krasno 1994; summarized in Gaddie and Bullock 2000: 35–36).

Despite extensively coding the prior political experience of candidates in his dataset, Canon (1990) adopts a four-point quality measure in his study of congressional races, including contests for open seats. Candidates with no prior elective office score one. Ambitious amateurs (identified on the basis of celebrity status, previous serious attempts for a congressional seat, and risk-taking in the primary election) score two; those with prior appointive experience score three; and four if the challenger has previous elective office (Canon 1990: Appendix B).

In their game theoretic analysis, Banks and Kiewiet (1989) assign challengers in the 1980–1984 elections to one of three categories: Strong challengers (those with prior elective office), weak challengers (those with no previous political experience); and to a "medium strength category" that includes all challengers who had either been congressional staffers, party officials, or had previously held a non-elected public office.

Studying U.S. Senate challengers between 1980 and 1986, Squire (1989) develops a measure of quality based on a hierarchy among offices as suggested by established political office career ladders. Squire argues that this simple scale captures much of what is meant by candidate quality but fine-tunes the measure by incorporating the percentage of a state's population represented or governed by a candidate to correct for the possibility of unfairly penalizing House members from large states. Squire devises a second measure of quality that constrains a representative's score between 300 and 500. In later work on U.S. Senate elections,

Squire (1992) similarly constructs a multiplicative measure that ranges from zero (no current political office) to 600 (incumbent governor).

Finally, several other studies use alternative measures. In his study of U.S. Senate elections between 1952 and 2000, Lublin (1994) breaks down Squire's hierarchy of offices into a set of six dummy variables and constructs an ordinal zero to four-point scale based on prior elective experience. In their study of U.S. House elections, Buttice and Stone (2012) used a 2006 survey of 9,000 constituents nationwide to estimate voter perceptions of House candidate quality, calculated as difference in experience on a five-point scale and difference in quality (defined with seven traits) on a seven-point scale. Finally, Praino, Stockemer, and Moscardelli (2013) used a three-point scale, closely adapting the standard dichotomous variable to a three-point scale, adding the category of "former U.S. representative." These measures aside, the lion's share of studies since 2000 noted in Table 2.1, have used the dichotomous measure to conceptualize challenger quality.

Despite considerable theoretical and conceptual debate over candidate quality measures, some comfort can be taken from the fact that the various measures almost always work as the theory predicts, producing results that are both statistically and substantively important (Squire 1995): Better candidates (as assessed by any measure) perform better. These results notwithstanding, Fowler (1993) argues that controversy over quality measurement limits the conclusions we can draw from the literature. Her work takes issue with the fact that none of the indices attempts to specify the intervals between categories of candidates, even though they are used in statistical analyses as if they are cardinal measures. There is also no control for regional variation in the importance of various kinds of experiences and none of the measures encompasses potentially relevant non-experiential qualities (ambition, energy, empathy, and policy concerns) (Fowler 1993: 113).

Fowler contends that no study has seriously attempted to assess tradeoffs involved with various measures of quality (1993: 113). (Gaddie and Bullock (2000) express a preference for the Green–Krasno measure in their work, claiming that it performs better in their analyses of open seat races, but do not evaluate other scholars' measures.) Nevertheless, Jacobson (1990) reports a 0.8 correlation between his measure and the Green–Krasno formulation.

As the debate over measuring candidate quality persists, the existing scholarly research supports the basic premise that some candidates are better than others. Accepting this assertion, we can consider an equally important question: What factors contribute to the emergence of quality candidates?

The Emergence of Quality Challengers

The "strategic politicians" thesis summarized in Chapter 1 suggests that quality challengers will not emerge randomly. Strategic politicians examine a host of institutional, structural, and subjective factors when considering a run for

Congress (Herrnson 1995: 36). Herrnson (1995) identifies a variety of potentially relevant considerations. Institutional factors may include filing deadlines, campaign finance laws, election procedures, and party rules. Structural factors taken into consideration may include the social, economic, and partisan composition of the district, geographic compactness, media markets, overlap between the district and lower-level electoral constituency, and the possibilities for advancement to alternative offices (Herrnson 1995). Contextual factors including electoral laws and party support also play significant roles in the decision to run against an incumbent (Carson and Roberts 2014).

Strategic behavior dictates that potential candidates will also assess the broader political climate in evaluating the costs and benefits of a possible run for Congress. Above all, potential contestants will take into account the likelihood of victory, which may depend, among other factors, on national political conditions (Jacobson 1989; Jacobson and Kernell 1981) and local factors (Bond, Covington, and Fleisher 1985; Krasno and Green 1988). Together, some combination of these factors will likely determine whether or not a quality challenger will emerge to challenge an incumbent.

To determine the incumbent's degree of vulnerability, prospective challengers identify and assess both national conditions and district-level conditions (Jacobson 1989; Jacobson and Kernell 1981). For Jacobson (1990), and in work with Sam Kernell (Jacobson and Kernell 1981), local conditions include the percentage of votes previously won by the candidate of the challenger's party, and whether or not the seat switched party hands in the previous election; national conditions include the economy and presidential approval (typically, a "party of administration" variable is added as a control) (Jacobson 1989). Together these local and national conditions will determine the probability that a high-quality challenger will oppose the incumbent.

Jacobson conducts both aggregate and district-level analyses to test the independent effects of each of these variables on challenger quality (Jacobson 1989). He also estimates these models separately for both Democratic and Republican candidates. Using data for congressional races between 1946 and 1986, Jacobson's district-level analysis demonstrates that both local and national conditions significantly affect the probability that a high-quality Democrat emerged to challenge a Republican. By contrast, Republican challengers seem to be sensitive only to local conditions. The coefficients for national variables do not achieve conventional significance levels for the Republican pool, despite the fact that they appear to be affecting the dependent variable in the anticipated direction (Jacobson 1989). His aggregate level analysis (for the same period) reveals similar results. Economic conditions and level of public approval for the president impact (positively) the overall level of high-quality Democratic—albeit not Republican—challengers. Jacobson concludes that Democratic challengers are "clearly more 'strategic'" than Republican challengers.

Other scholars find Jacobson's explanation incomplete and argue that additional, district-specific variables account for the emergence of high-quality challengers. Bond, Covington, and Fleisher (1985) conduct an individual-level analysis using data from candidates for Congress in 1980 to test for the effect of these variables. Their study finds support for these claims. They show that the strongest explanatory variables are measures of local partisan forces (the incumbent's vote in the previous election and the normal vote in the district). They also find support for national tides. Bond, Covington, and Fleisher also demonstrate that high-quality challengers are more likely to emerge against an incumbent when the latter's policy behavior is incongruent with the district's policy preferences (Bond, Covington, and Fleisher 1985). (They also found that the degree of district heterogeneity and incumbents' use of perks, such as advertising and casework, had no significant influence on the probability that a strong challenger would emerge.)

Still others argue that incumbents may be able to deter high-quality challengers through their fundraising and spending strategies and through the messages that fundraising successes—or failures—and spending levels may send to potential challengers (Epstein and Zemsky 1995). Ultimately, however, this study concludes that fundraising only minimally deters high-quality challengers, and that incumbent spending has no influence on a challenger's decision to enter a race (Epstein and Zemsky 1995).

In their recent study of candidate quality and electoral competition in congressional races from 1872–1944, Carson and Roberts (2014) find that congressional races during this era, despite having higher levels of quality challengers on average, closely mirror the structure of their contemporary counterparts. Using newly collected data on congressional races during this period, the authors were able to delineate electoral behavior during an era that scholars have examined much less than late 20th-century politics. They posit that the high success rate of challengers during this era can be attributed to the successful recruiting of quality challengers by opposition parties (Carson and Roberts 2014: 147).

In addition, Carson and Roberts (2014) find that the significant drop in a number of quality challengers in the early 20th century can be attributed to institutional reforms in the late 19th century such as the Australian ballot and direct primaries. These reforms limited parties' ability to produce quality challengers by driving up the entry risk of prospective candidates to enter races and, in turn, increased their selectiveness. These findings support previous conceptualizations of strategic politicians (Herrnson 1995) by attributing changes in patterns of quality candidate emergence to institutional reforms and not to changes in candidate behavior. In their work, Carson and Roberts (2014) discovered that experienced candidates calculated the entry risk of running in ways similar to contemporary politicians (Carson and Roberts 2014). Jacobson and Carson (2016) find similar patterns in challenger quality between 19th-century electoral politics and contemporary races. Prior to these electoral reforms, parties were able to convince high-quality candidates to run against strong incumbents with the promise of kickbacks and patronage (Jacobson and Carson 2016).

In his study of challengers in U.S. Senate elections between 1980 and 1986, Peverill Squire constructs models using alternative explanatory variables to predict the quality of a Senate challenger (Squire 1989). Squire finds similar results for both of his conceptualizations of quality (see above). Squire examines the effect of various personal and political characteristics of the incumbent and finds no significant effects. Squire's study tests for the impact of a key institutional variable—the size of the pool of high-quality candidates in a state—and finds that this measure substantially and significantly predicts the likelihood of a strong challenger emerging (Squire 1989). This finding is confirmed in later work in which Squire (with Adams) conducts an individual-level analysis of U.S. Senate races in 1992 (Adams and Squire 1997). In this study, the authors code challenger quality (the dependent variable) on a zero to 600 scale and use NES data which allows them to measure and to include a variety of additional independent variables, including voters' approval of the incumbent, the level of the incumbent's contact with voters, and the degree of the incumbent's visibility in the district. In the final analysis, only the size of the challenger pool has a significant (positive) effect (Adams and Squire 1997).

Lublin also studies challenger quality in U.S. Senate elections. Using individual-level data from elections between 1952 and 1990, Lublin measures the quality of a challenger on a zero to four scale. He conducts both an OLS and an ordered probit analysis to test for the effects of a variety of local and national political and economic variables. He finds that only senatorial constituency size and the year of the election fail to show a significant relationship to the dependent variable (Lublin 1994). The local and national variables all influence the quality of senatorial challengers. Lublin argues that national conditions dominate local factors. His results reveal that national economic conditions influence challenger quality nearly three times as much as state economic conditions (Lublin 1994).

Van Dunk also has investigated challenger quality in state legislative elections (Van Dunk 1997). She examines challenger quality in 819 state legislative races across ten states between 1988 and 1992. Her analysis uses the dichotomous measure of quality preferred by Jacobson. Van Dunk conducts a maximum likelihood/ logit analysis to estimate the probability that a challenger has held elected office. Her findings indicate that the likelihood of a high-quality challenger running is related to the incumbent's previous electoral appeal, the incumbent's personal characteristics (including age and legislative experience), state partisan conditions, and statewide economic conditions (Van Dunk 1997).

Drawing on rational choice theory, Banks and Kiewiet offer a different conceptualization based on the conventional equation of political participation:

$$R = p \star B - C + D$$

They argue that the utility of engaging in the political act (in this case, running against an incumbent), R, equals the benefits (B) that accrue from the act (being elected to Congress) times the probability that (p) that the act will yield the benefit, minus the cost (C) of engaging in the act, plus the private consumption value (D) of the act (Riker and Ordeshook 1973; Banks and Kiewiet 1989). Banks and Kiewiet thus incorporate theoretically the costs of running for office as well as the private consumption benefits—*in addition* to the probability of winning—into the strategic calculus potential challengers will use to determine whether or not to challenge an incumbent. Their analysis goes on to suggest that high-quality incumbents differ in significant ways from weak incumbents who evaluate the same conditions while deciding whether to challenge an incumbent. They argue that weak challengers may not assess conditions as accurately as high-quality challengers, that weak challengers have less to lose, and that running even under unfavorable circumstances may increase low-quality challengers' chances of future success. In short, they argue that it is not irrational for weak challengers to run against incumbents even when strong challengers opt out (Banks and Kiewiet 1989).

David Canon's (1990) work has made valuable contributions to scholars' understanding of the factors that impact the likelihood that quality challengers will emerge. His research examines the effect of numerous variables on challenger quality in elections for the U.S. House and the U.S. Senate and on candidate quality in open seat races. Canon's model includes short-term district-level (incumbent's previous vote, freshman members, age, and scandals) as well as national-level variables (real disposable personal income, state unemployment level, and a control for Watergate). Canon also tests for the effect of a variety of structural and institutional variables including turnover rates, the "shape" of the structure of political careers (clearly defined stepping-stones to higher office), the supply of experienced candidates, the normal vote for the incumbent, the type of nominating system (active versus inactive party involvement), institutionalized practices (endorsements, number of candidates in the primary), and redistricting. (For obvious reasons, some variables cannot be included in the Senate model.)

Canon finds that most variables perform as expected in his models. In the probit model that estimates the probability that a quality challenger will emerge in a U.S. House race, all of the district-level variables (except age) increase the probability that a quality challenger would emerge. National variables indicate that the Watergate dummies strongly predict experience. All four of the economic variables exert statistically significant effects, with unemployment having the largest impact. With respect to structural variables, Canon finds that redistricting was the most significant variable in the model; incumbents hurt by redistricting are virtually guaranteed to face an experienced challenger (the probability increases by 39%). While political parties, through their endorsement practices and their ability to restrict the field of candidates did exert influence on the level of experience, variables pertinent to voter participation were insignificant at conventional levels (Canon 1990: 105–106).

Canon finds that most variables perform well in the open seats model, but he notes some key differences. National-level variables (real income, unemployment, and Watergate) do not appear to influence the likelihood that quality candidates will enter open seat races. By contrast, all of the district-level variables and several structural variables (challenger's normal vote, redistricting, the shape of the opportunity structure (for Republicans) the supply of candidates, and the party's ability to restrict the field of candidates) exert the anticipated effects (Canon 1990: 108).

In the Senate model, Canon (1990) finds that only the previous challenger's vote, the normal vote, freshman status, and whether or not the incumbent was involved in a scandal were significant predictors of experience.

In general, Canon's (1990) findings support the expectations generated by the strategic politicians theory. Canon's work makes two special contributions to the literature in this field. First, Canon demonstrates the importance of a variety of structural and institutional factors. He argues that "the structural variables are a significant contribution to our understanding of the factors that frame the context of the decision to run ... [They] emphasize the importance of the *context* of choice and the rules of the game" (Canon 1990: 110). Second, Canon's comprehensive approach, studying both U.S. House and U.S. Senate races as well as open seat races, yields some compelling evidence that the influence of various factors may not be consistent across institutions and types of races.

Gronke's (2001) pioneering study takes this approach a step further. Challenging received wisdom that dramatic differences exist between House and Senate campaigns, Gronke (2001) argues that there are fewer differences than previous research may have led scholars to believe. Arguing that, "[i]t is not useful to think about the Senate and House as distinct archetypes," (2001: 10), Gronke presses for—and develops—a unified approach to studying elections across the chambers in such a way that, "amplifies the ways in which the House and Senate differ and the ways in which they are converging" (11).

Gronke (2001) devotes substantial attention to candidate quality in his study. His findings offer strong support for the strategic politicians thesis, demonstrating that challenger quality is most related to measures of competitiveness (partisan balance and closeness) rather than political setting. Gronke's work makes at least two main contributions to the literature on challenger quality. First, Gronke develops a set of hypotheses and tests for the impact of a variety of key variables (such as media market efficiency and district heterogeneity) that had not previously been considered systematically in models to predict quality. Even as most of these variables (summarized in Table 2.2) did exert significant influence, Gronke makes strong theoretical arguments about why they are relevant in such models and presents some preliminary results about their impact.

Gronke's second contribution is that he offers some evidence about institutional differences with respect to challenger quality. Despite previous research in this area that may suggest otherwise (Krasno 1994), Gronke observes no institutional differences once he incorporates the appropriate controls (2001). To be sure, Gronke, like other scholars (Krasno 1994), observes a large gap in challenger

TABLE 2.2 Emergence of Quality Challenger—Summary

Source	Period	Dependent Variable	Independent Variables
Bianco (1984)	1974	Challenger Experience: Dichotomous	Challenger's party; Real disposable income (by state/1 year in advance of filing); Previous challenger's margin; Presidential vote (four year avg.); Watergate; Retiring incumbent's party.
Jacobson (1990)	1946–1988	Challenger Experience: Dichotomous	Real disposable income (second qtr/second qtr); Presidential approval (avg. April–June); Administration's party; Previous Democratic vote; Previous party control; Candidate pool.
	1946–1988	% Experienced Challengers	Real disposable income (second qtr/second qtr); Presidential approval (avg. April–June); Administration's party; Previous % Democratic win.
Bond, Covington, and Fleischer (1985)	1980	Challenger Experience: Two ways: Three-point scale; Composite	Incumbent previous vote; incumbent's party; Normal vote; District diversity; Incumbent's ideological differences; Advertisment/casework.
Krasno and Green (1988)	1974–1988	Challenger Experience: Nine-point scale (0–8)	Previous challenger's vote; Party dummy; Scandal; Incumbent money.
Squire (1989)	1980–1986	Challenger Experience: Two ways: Seven-point ordinal scale (0–6); 300–500 point scale	Incumbent's seniority; Incumbent age; Incumbent previous vote × ideological distance; Incumbent primary margin; Challenger's party; Size of quality pool; Midterm election dummy; State Population (log); Challenger party strength.
Canon (1990)	1972–1988	Challenger Experience: Four-point scale (1–4)	Real disposable income (by state/one year in advance of filing); Previous challenger's margin; State unemployment; Normal vote; Watergate; Scandal; Open primary; Redistricting; Institutions (4); Challenger's age; incumbent freshman.
Lublin (1994)	1952–1990	Challenger Experience: Five-point scale (0–4)	Previous incumbent vote; Change in Presidential approval; Incumbent of President's party; Change in real PCI by state; Change in real PCI nationwide; Number of congressional districts; Year dummy.

(Continued)

TABLE 2.2 (*Continued*)

Source	Period	Dependent Variable	Independent Variables
Adams and Squire (1997)	1992	Challenger Experience: 0–600 point scale	Challenger pool; Ideological difference; Incumbent vote % (1996); Incumbent approval (1990); Incumbent 1990 approval-1988 approval, Incumbent contact with voters, Incumbent visibility with voters; State population (log).
Van Dunk (1997)	(1988–1992)	Challenger Dichotomous	Incumbent previous vote; Change in per capita income (state); Legislative competition; Legislative compensation; Incumbent age; Incumbent legislative experience.
Gronke (2001)	1982–1996	Challenger Experience: Four-point scale (1–4)	Model 1: Closeness; Partisan balance; Contiguity; Dominance; Income variance; Education variance; Racial diversity; Urbanness; Foreign stock; Institution (House/Senate). Model 2: Incumbent ideological extremity; Age of member; Seniority of member; Vote (t-1); Institution. Model 3: All variables from Model 1 and Model 2.
Cox and Katz (2002)	1946–1998	Entry by Experienced Challenger: Dichotomous	Model 1: Lagged incumbent vote; Lagged incumbency status; Open seat, Unforeseeably open. Model 2: Lagged incumbent vote; Lagged incumbency status; Number of districts in state; State redrawn. (Non-south only.)
Carson and Roberts (2005)	1975–2000	Entry by Experienced Challenger and Reaction from Incumbent. Four possible outcomes: Experienced Challenger runs and Incumbent Retires; EC runs and incumbent seeks reelection; EC does not run and incumbent retires; EC does not run and incumbent runs.	Percent incumbent supported party position on key roll call votes; % of two-party vote in previous election; % of two-party vote for presidential candidate of incumbent; Incumbent spending in previous election; Incumbent status in party; Incumbent seniority; Redistricting years; Status as minority party; Incumbent partisan score.

(*Continued*)

TABLE 2.2 (*Continued*)

Source	Period	Dependent Variable	Independent Variables
Carson and Roberts (2014)	1872–1990	Entry by Experienced Challenger: Dichotomous	Model 1: Democratic % of two-party vote; Incumbent running; Party defending seat; Congressional majority. Model 2: Lagged Democratic vote %; Incumbent running; Party defending seat; Congressional majority; Change in GNP; Change in GNP interacted with majority status. Model 3: Repeats Model 1 with dummy for direct primary.
Pyeatt (2014)	1954–2008	Experienced Challenger: Dichotomous	Model 1: Ideological extremity; District ideology; Freshman; Gender; Change in Income; Incumbent voteshare (prior election); Incumbent majority party; presidential approval rate; Midterm dummy. Model 2: Same as model, plus interaction between ideological extremity and district ideology.
Barnes, Branton, and Cassese (2017)	1994–2004	Experienced Challenger Success: Dichotomous	Gender; Quality opponent; Gender-quality interaction; In-party seat; Women friendly district dummy; % Women in state legislature; Closed primary dummy; Redistricting dummy; Annual fixed effects.
Arceneaux, Dunaway, Johnson, and Vander Wielen (2020)	1998–2010	Entry by Experienced Challenger: Dichotomous	% District voters receive Fox News; Democratic support; Party unity; Sending gap; Freshman; President's party dummy; Midterm dummy; Change in GDP; Lagged incumbent voteshare.
Sparks (2020)	2012–2018	Entry by Experienced Challenger: Dichotomous	One-party Contests dummy; Incumbent terms in office; Incumbent ideology; Incumbent warchest; Incumbent previous win margin; One-party contest (lagged); One-party contest × incumbent previous win margin interaction; Challenger party strength; Incumbent party; State dummy.

Source: Fowler (1993); Post-1993 studies summarized by author.

quality between House and Senate (1.5 points on the Canon/four-point scale he employs; see Gronke (2001), Table 4.2). However, after he controls for district diversity and competitiveness, the gap is reduced by half (0.76). Further controls for incumbent characteristics and electoral environment reduce the gap to about one-tenth (0.16) and render it statistically insignificant. Testing a series of specifications, reestimating models in separate years, separately for institutions and fully dummied versions, the results remain robust and consistent in their impact. Institutions remained insignificant in all polled analyses, specified either as a separate dummy variable or as an interaction term (Gronke 2001: 98). Gronke concludes from these results that, "House/Senate differences in challenger quality are a product of differences in the competitive nature of states, the high level of media market efficiency of states, and the ideological position and previous electoral performance of Senate incumbents, not anything distinctively attractive about the Senate as an institution" (2001: 100). Gronke claims that his findings, "fundamentally change the way political science describes, and theorizes about, differences in campaigning across these two institutions" (2001: 98).

In their (2002) study, Cox and Katz trace the presence (or lack thereof) of an experienced challenger in a contested race against an incumbent partly to the effects of redistricting. Guided by Jaconson and Kernell's strategic politicians reasoning, Cox and Katz explore how redistricting affected incumbents' "prudential exits and challengers' strategic entries" (2002: 6). They argue that redistrictings, once rare and often unforeseeable, became unavoidable and regular after several key reapportionment decisions by the Supreme Court in the 1960s. This knowledge facilitated better coordination between incumbents and strong challengers (2002: 7). Their findings show that experienced challengers became more likely to bide their time, waiting for the incumbent to depart before launching their own candidacies (2002: 149). Cox and Katz also provide evidence that strong challengers are more likely to enter just after redistricting (2002: 166). Controlling for the normal vote in the district, the number of terms served by the incumbent, the number of districts in the state, and year effects, Cox and Katz (2002) show that incumbents have been more likely to exit and strong challengers have been more likely to enter in the election immediately following redistricting since the Supreme Court's 1966 *Wesberry v. Sanders* reapportionment decision (170).

Several recent studies have built on these findings, comparing new variables such as ideology, gender, news exposure, and state level reforms. Pyeatt (2014) used Jacobson's dataset to test the effects of incumbent ideology on the likelihood of facing a quality challenger in U.S. House and U.S. Senate elections between 1954 and 2008. The author found that ideologically extreme incumbents from districts with similarly extreme ideologies, tend not to face quality challengers.

Further, Barnes, Branton, and Cassese (2017) examined U.S. House races with quality candidates between 1994 and 2004. They found that when Republican women with experience faced experienced opponents, they were 31% less likely to win than their male opponents. In contrast, for Democrats, the odds were even when facing a single quality challenger, Democratic experienced women facing multiple quality opponents were 14% less likely to win than their male colleagues, illustrating a potential gender bias from voters.

Later, Arceneaux, Dunaway, Johnson, and Vander Wielen (2020) examined a natural experiment of as-if random rollout to Fox News reception between 2008 and 2010. They found that voters' exposure to Fox News boosted the likelihood of Democratic incumbents facing a quality challenger, although the effect was weaker in districts with greater levels of Democratic support.

Finally, Sparks (2020) examined U.S. House races in California and Washington between 2012 and 2018. These states reformed elections to allow for two, same-party candidates to face off in general elections. The authors found that, after these reforms, incumbents were more likely to face a quality challenger from the same party than the opposing party, compared to before.

These four studies (Pyeatt 2014; Barnes, Branton, and Cassese 2017; Arceneaux et al. 2019; Sparks 2020) highlight that ideology, gender, news exposure, and institutional reforms can shape the likelihood that experienced candidates emerge in U.S. House races, but each focused on narrow time periods, with Pyeatt (2014) ending in 2008 while the other three studies began no earlier than 1994. Closer attention is needed to detail the main drivers of candidate quality *over time*.

One general criticism of the literature on candidate quality is that most studies analyze only actual candidacies and largely exclude the systematic study of prospective candidates (Fowler 1993). Scholars have begun to address this shortcoming in the literature and to devote greater attention to assessing prospective candidates, regardless of whether or not they declare candidacy (Maisel et al. 2001). Maisel's and his colleagues' Candidate Emergence Studies augment scholarship in this area by focusing on the "non-event: strong potential candidates who decide not to run" (Maisel et al. 2001: 33). The authors find similarities between these potential high-quality candidates and actual high-quality candidates. Many potential candidates' strategic calculations, for instance, are influenced by the probability of victory and the costs of running (Maisel 2000). There is widespread optimism that sustained research in this area will produce fruitful results while closing important gaps in the research agenda.

Despite the rich literature on challenger quality and candidate emergence, many questions remain unanswered. Moreover, scholars' lack of consensus about methodological issues and substantive findings may limit the conclusions we can draw from the literature about relevant aspects of candidate quality and emergence. "Has the strategic politicians literature been a dead end, given so many contradictory and inconclusive results?" asks Fowler, rhetorically (1993: 107). "I think not," Fowler adds, "for it has been an area of research that looks remarkably like real science, if once excuses the absence of genuine replication" (1993:107).

Yet scholarly debate over many aspects related to candidacy has obscured many important considerations. Fowler warns that

> the last decade has sparked a variety of inquiries that bring us closer to understanding the myriad ways in which candidacy affects congressional elections, but in doing so, it has revealed how much more remains unknown. Before the ambiguous status of candidacy is resolved, many methodological issues require attention. Furthermore, many of the parameters we recognize as influencing candidate decision-making are in a state of flux. These circumstances create opportunities for new research while at the same time they lend a certain urgency to the investigative enterprise. If scholars fail to understand candidate emergence in the present context, they may limit their capacity to explain it in the future.
>
> *(1993: 119)*

Fowler's remarks make clear that, while researchers have yielded many useful insights about candidate quality, much remains to be investigated. She also reiterates her contention that the literature needs to place greater emphasis on exploring developments over time. It is the task of this book to advance such an undertaking in the chapters that follow.

3
EXPLAINING CHALLENGER QUALITY
Hypotheses and Methodology

The literature summarized in the previous chapter demonstrates that scholars have labored extensively to identify factors that are associated with the emergence of experienced challengers in congressional elections. Despite the fact that many of these studies examine challenger quality over a substantial period of time, few analyses have advanced serious attempts to consider developments in the explanatory factors and their consequences over similar periods (See Chapter 1 for discussion). The remainder of this book undertakes this task in an effort to explain patterns in challenger quality.

The analyses that follow are based in the rational actor tradition of candidacy that treats decisions to run for office as the relatively straightforward and familiar calculation of costs and benefits discounted by the perceived probability of winning (Fowler 1993: 60; Black 1972; Levine and Hyde 1977; Rohde 1979; Brace 1984; Abramson, Aldrich, and Rohde 1987; Bank and Kiewiet 1989). This approach yields the following expected utility model:

$$U(O) = p(B) - (1-p)C$$

The model predicts that individuals will run if $U(O)$ is positive, most likely to be the case when the estimated probability of success (p) is high, when the perceived benefits of the office (B) are high, and/or when the costs of losing (C) are low (summarized from Fowler 1993: 60). Fowler has also put it differently: "Alternatively, one can argue that a positive outcome occurs when candidates are tolerant of risk and do not require a 'fair' lottery to induce them to run" (Fowler 1979; Fowler 1993: 60). Either way, Fowler claims, the logic of the decision is the same (Fowler 1993: 60).

For the most part, scholarship in this area has not focused evenly on all of the components of the cost-benefit model. Fowler (1993) argues that "[r]ational choice scholars ... have been inattentive to parameters other than the p term. The size of the B term, for example, is a key component of these models, but theorists have not controlled for the factors that might cause it to vary. The same criticism applies to variation in the C term" (Fowler 1993: 60).

I argue that we can observe social, political, and institutional developments that have contributed to variation in the p, B, and C terms, and that these changes can help to explain the decline in challenger quality between 1972 and 2000.

Before attempting to account for the decline in challenger quality during this period (see Chapter 9), however, it is necessary to establish clear relationships between a variety of factors and challenger quality. To that end, I will develop and test a variety of empirical models to predict the emergence of an experienced challenger in contested elections for the U.S. House. The first model will explain variations in the aggregate level of challenger quality in each cycle during this period. The second model is a district(individual)-level model to predict the probability that a high-quality challenger emerges.

The previous chapter demonstrates that scholars account for variation in challenger quality based on a variety of national and district-level factors, as well as institutional and structural variables. I will consider the impact of factors which I believe are related to the key terms in the equation above but that have been largely excluded from consideration in the literature. Specifically, I will consider the effects of campaign costs, the "benefits" of office, and the impact of state legislative term limits. I will also include two other factors in the analysis: electoral competition and redistricting. I develop hypotheses and expectations with respect to each below.

Challenger Quality and "the 'p' Term"

Fowler (1993) argues that researchers who have probed determinants of challenger quality have focused disproportionately on "the 'p' term" in their cost-benefit analyses. This term typically reflects an assessment about the likelihood of winning, or, in rational choice language, of attaining the desired benefit once the cost has been assumed. Scholars conceptualize this term in a variety of ways, arguing that potential candidates allow national-level and district-level variables to influence their perceptions of the probability of winning. Chapter 2 reveals that such factors as presidential approval, economic conditions, and incumbents' prior electoral performance are among the variables considered to be related to this probability (see Chapter 2 for additional details).

Previous research asserts that measures of *competitiveness* are reasonable indicators that affect perceptions about the probability of winning. Consequently, I contend that electoral competitiveness is a key determinant of challenger quality. The analyses that follow will incorporate measures of competitiveness and their impact on the variables of interest. Consistent with previous research, I hypothesize that lower levels of competitiveness will depress overall challenger quality and reduce the likelihood that a high-quality challenger emerges against an incumbent.

Some studies suggest competition in congressional elections is declining (Jacobson 2000), while the incumbency advantage may be mounting, a finding that has emerged across a variety of alternative conceptualizations of incumbency advantage (Mayhew 1974; Erikson 1971; King and Gelman 1991). With more than 90% of candidates being incumbents and more than 90% of them winning, empirical studies show that incumbents have dominated postwar elections for the U.S. House, winning reelection at both consistent rates and at large margins (Jacobson 1990). On average, less than 2% of all incumbents are defeated in the primary and less than 7% lose in general elections (Jacobson 1990). Incumbents enjoy advantages that include gerrymandered districts (Cover 1977), high name recognition (Mayhew 1974), professional staff (Jacobson 1990), opportunities to provide constituent service (Serra and Moon 1994), superior fundraising ability (Ansolabehere and Snyder 2000; Jacobson 2000), franking privileges (Jacobson 2000; Mayhew 1974), and credit claiming (Mayhew 1974.)

Scholars assert that *redistricting* contributes to declining competitiveness. Pro-incumbent gerrymandering that tends to yield more safe seats than competitive districts has been blamed for contributing to the rising success of incumbents since the late 1960s (Davidson and Oleszek 2004: 50). In keeping with expectations in previous work (Canon 1990; Cox and Katz 2002), I control for the effects of redistricting in this study. Specifically, I hypothesize that redistricting will positively impact overall levels of challenger quality and heighten the probability that a high-quality contender challenges an incumbent.

The hypotheses I will test with respect to the "p" term (in the cost-benefits calculation potential candidates are assumed to undertake when deciding whether or not to run against an incumbent) are largely consistent with most of the literature associated with this question. I believe these are important factors that affect candidates' calculations about the probability of winning. Details about how each of these factors is conceptualized for the analyses that follow are provided in subsequent chapters.

Challenger Quality and "the 'B' Term"

While factors that influence perceptions about the probability of winning (the "p" term) have dominated analyses of challenger quality, less attention has been devoted to the other components of the equation (Fowler 1993). I claim that factors relevant to the benefits perceived to be associated with electoral victory also affect the decision to run against an incumbent and that greater attention should be paid to evaluating the impact of factors related to this "B" term.

Previous studies have recognized the importance of factors related to the perceived benefits of holding office, but few of these studies have systematically examined the impact of such factors on challenger quality. Canon (1990) suggests that the "desirability of office" is an important factor and that it represents a "promising avenue for exploration" (69). Canon contends that "[t]he desirability of an office clearly has an effect on the type of candidate recruited to that office" (69). Even though Canon identifies this factor as an important one for the decision-making calculus, few studies proceed to operationalize "desirability" (or any other factor related to perceived benefits of winning a congressional seat) as a variable and to investigate its impact on challenger quality levels.

This book recognizes the relevance of factors related to the perceived benefits of attaining office and will examine the impact of these factors in the analyses that follow. Details about how I operationalize these factors follow (see Chapters 6 and 8). I hypothesize that stronger perceptions about the benefits of holding congressional office correspond with attracting greater proportions of high-quality challengers and increase the likelihood that high-quality challengers emerge.

Challenger Quality and "the 'C' Term"

Few developments with respect to the politics of congressional elections over the past three decades have been as pronounced as the changes in the costs of a campaign. Campaign costs—and, correspondingly, candidates' expenditures—have increased dramatically during this period (Magleby 2002; Jacobson 2000). (Chapter 4 provides a more comprehensive discussion about rising campaign costs and candidate expenditures.) Even as the costs associated with a run against an incumbent are a critical component of the cost-benefit calculation, no study to my knowledge has incorporated measures of campaign costs in models to explain or predict challenger quality.

I believe that tests of a complete model of the cost-benefit calculation described above need to incorporate campaign finance considerations. I hypothesize that as the amount of financial resources necessary to mount a congressional campaign against an incumbent grows (in other words, as campaign costs rise), the overall level of challenger quality will drop. Increased campaign costs are also hypothesized to depress the likelihood that a high-quality contender will challenge an incumbent. I also consider alternative possibilities.

Structural and Institutional Factors and Challenger Quality

Previous studies show that both national-level and district-level factors are related to challenger quality (Jacobson 1990; Bond, Covington, and Fleisher 1985; Lublin 1994; see Chapter 2 for details and additional citations). Scholars have also examined the impact of a variety of structural and institutional factors measured at the state level that appear to be related to challenger quality. Redistricting (Canon 1990), size of the candidate pool (Squire 1989; Adams and Squire 1997), and number of congressional districts (Lublin 1994) are among these factors. There remain a variety of additional state-level factors that are not systematically examined in previous work.

Canon (1990) suggests that state legislative professionalization affects challenger quality. He argues that "increasing professionalization of state legislatures [is likely to] recruit more candidates with ambition for higher office" (1990: 70). He does not explicitly test this supposition in any of his models, however. Alternatively, Fowler and McClure (1989) argue that state legislative professionalization may have the opposite effect. Satisfied with greater opportunities closer to home, Fowler and McClure suggest there may be a tendency for members of more professionalized state legislators to remain at home rather than to run for Congress (1989). What little evidence exists in the literature about the effect of state legislative professionalization on challenger quality is mixed, at best, with serious questions about the generalizability of the findings (Canon 1990; Fowler and McClure 1989; Squire 1988). The hypothesis implied by Fowler and McClure, however, seems reasonable, and I will test it in the analyses that follow. Specifically, I expect that challenger quality in states with more professionalized state legislatures will be lower than in states in which legislatures are less professionalized.

Canon (1990) also suggests that the strength of a state's political party system may impact challenger quality. "Change in a party's success at the polls is the surest way to alter the nature of political opportunity," Canon posits (1990: 70). We may reasonably expect that where two-party competition is greater, each party will have greater success in recruiting high-quality candidates. I hypothesize, thus, that stronger two-party competition has a positive effect on quality.

More contemporary studies have found additional links between institutional configuration and challenger quality. Carson et al. (2011) discovered that congruence between state legislative district and congressional district can increase the probability of a high-quality challenger in that congressional district from the state legislature. Carson and Roberts (2014) showed that regulations of political parties and oversight can dictate political parties' ability to recruit high-quality candidates and challengers. Their study of institutional reforms at the turn of the 20th century contends that alterations to the rules dictating candidate selection caused a significant drop in the number of quality challengers in the following years after the reforms.

The literature on this subject is largely silent on the effect of one recent institutional development, however: State legislative term limits. I hypothesize that state legislative term limits should exert a positive effect on the overall level of quality challengers. State legislative term limits should also increase the likelihood that high-quality challengers emerge against incumbents. Chapter 5 presents a more elaborate discussion of state legislative term limits and its impact on candidate quality and electoral competition more generally. This chapter also presents some initial evidence on the impact of state legislative term limits on challenger quality. Subsequent analyses incorporate state legislative term limits as a factor in the multivariate models (to be described below.)

Some scholarship focuses on the relationship between redistricting and challenger quality (Cox and Katz 2002). Theoretically, the impact of redistricting is complex. New to the officeholder, redrawn districts may be perceived to reduce an incumbent's advantages, suggesting that redistricting should encourage stronger incumbent opposition. We also know, however, that legislative redistricting is often guided by incumbent protection schemes that may discourage serious contenders (Mayhew 1971; King and Gelman 1991; Cain 1984; Owen and Grofman 1988.)

This study will examine the impact of each of these state-level, structural, or institutional factors on challenger quality in congressional elections. Chapter 7 will present the results of state-level analyses that incorporate these factors, and Chapter 8 will incorporate these factors in a complete, individual-level model.

Methodology: Models and Tests

A more comprehensive theoretical model to explain challenger quality must incorporate each of the factors mentioned above. To examine the impact of each factor more systematically, I develop and empirically test several models in the chapters that follow. In Chapter 8, I will also test the hypotheses introduced above and described in greater detail using district-level models to predict the probability that a high-quality challenger will emerge against an incumbent using data from 1972 to 2018.

In all of these analyses, I opt for the operationalization of quality preferred by Jacobson (and Jacobson and Kernell 1981). That is, I utilize a dichotomous conceptualization of quality based only on whether or not the challenger has held prior elective office. Despite the scholarly debate over quality measurement (summarized in Chapter 2), the original formulation offered by Jacobson remains commonly used in the literature and maintains solid explanatory ability (Jacobson 2000). Despite its status as the cruder measure of quality, the dichotomous formulation remains a useful approximation. (Jacobson reports a correlation of 0.80 between his measure of quality and the Krasno and Green (1988) measure (Jacobson 1990).) Moreover, Fowler (1993) suggests that "disagreements between authors [about quality measurement] have major consequences for ... widely divergent findings ... [I]nformation regarding relationships between rival indices for other years is unavailable, and comparisons among other scales are nonexistent" (114).

As scholars have continued to examine the issue of challenger quality, they have seemingly become more devoted to this measure. Most recent works on the subject, including Carson (2005), Carson et al. (2011), Carson and Roberts (2014), and Jacobson and Carson (2016), have continued to utilize this conception of challenger quality in their studies. "Indeed this simple dichotomous measure consistently outperforms more nuanced measure of quality that seek to differentiate levels of office or types of background experience" (Carson and Roberts 2014: 31). By using the Jacobson measure of quality I aim to use the measure most readily available, most commonly used by scholars, and generally regarded as the most acceptable in order to advance my claims.

Explaining the Decline in Challenger Quality: Hypotheses

The empirical models I will estimate in Chapters 6 and 8 will test the expectations described above about the relationship between the various factors and the emergence of experienced challengers in contested races against congressional incumbents. In the end, however, this book seeks to explain the dynamics of challenger quality we observe over this period. More specifically, the analyses will help to explain the decline in challenger quality we observe.

I hypothesize that the decline in challenger quality between 1972 and 2018 can be explained by escalating campaign costs. An alternative hypothesis is that challenger quality has declined during this period because competitiveness in congressional races has dropped significantly.

Hypothesis 3.1: Fewer high-quality candidates are contesting incumbents in congressional elections because the cost of campaigns has been increasing.

Hypothesis 3.2: Fewer high-quality candidates are contesting incumbents in congressional races because districts have become less competitive.

To understand why challenger quality has declined, I will show that the levels of the key explanatory determinants (campaign costs and competitiveness) have changed. Specifically, I will provide evidence that campaign costs have increased and that competitiveness has declined during this period.

4
MONEY AND CHALLENGER QUALITY

Spending in congressional campaigns has grown exponentially over the past half century. Consider that overall spending for congressional races nationwide has increased 15-fold (controlling for inflation) since the 1970s, from approximately $60 million in 1976 to over $929 million in 2010. Figure 4.1 presents average campaign expenditures by candidate type for each election cycle between 1972 and 2018. Spending has increased in every category. In 1974, the average challenger who defeated an incumbent spent $533,312; by 2018, the average successful challenger spent $5,878,376 (See Figure 4.1; Table 4.1).

Why has campaign spending increased so dramatically? The simple story is that campaigns have become more and more expensive. Scholars trace the escalating costs of campaigns to a number of factors. Explanations include the growth in the voting age population (up 39% since 1974), resulting in candidates' need to communicate with more voters, and the changing means and conditions of effective campaigning (DiClerico 2000). Candidates must increasingly rely on expensive campaign communications mechanisms, broadcast television and radio advertisements, and direct mail. Furthermore, as the number of broadcast media channels has increased, voters' attention to politics decreased, and the impact of persuasive media dwindled, campaigns have been required to consistently augment their overall investments in advertising over time.

Rising advertising costs—especially broadcast advertising on television—are likely to be at least partly responsible for rendering political campaigns more expensive over time. Television advertisements have become the predominant communications medium for candidates for the U.S. Congress. Darrell West (1994) claims that commercials have become the major strategic tool for contesting elections in America and finds that candidates devote the largest share of their

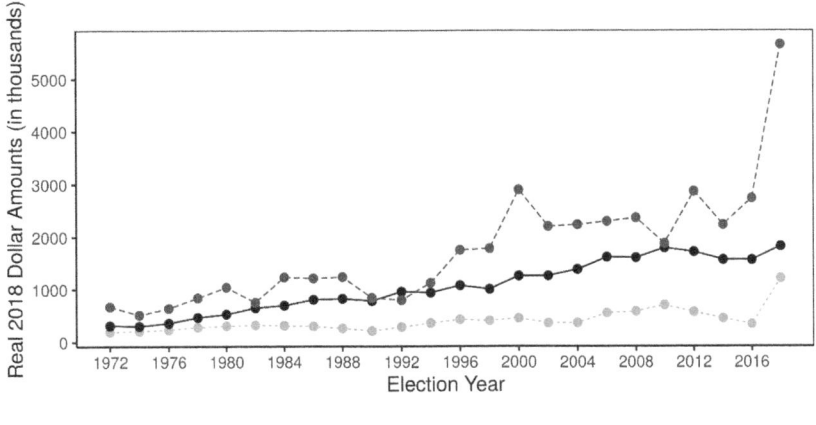

FIGURE 4.1 Average Campaign Expenditures by Candidate (General Election) (1972–2018)

overall campaign budgets to television advertising. In fact, the typical candidate will reserve over 40% of the campaign budget for television advertising (West 1994). West (1994) argues that television ads are effective at informing voters. His (1994) study reveals that voters learn more about issues from television advertisements than from the news. He also finds that television ads influence how voters learn about candidates, what issues voters identify as priorities, what standards voters use to assess candidates, and how voters attribute blame (West 1994). These findings suggest it would not be an overstatement to view television political advertisements as the primary communications vehicle in contemporary congressional campaigns.

Several developments have made television advertisements increasingly expensive in recent decades. First, traditional television audiences are dwindling. Second, analysts believe audiences to be increasingly selective with respect to exposure and retention to advertising messages. The average number of broadcasts required in order to make an impression on the average viewer is estimated to have jumped from three to 17 over the past few years. At the same time, prices are on the rise. The average cost of a 30-second network television ad during primetime rose from $25,100 in 1972 to $111,500 in 2012 (in real dollars). This amounts to a significant escalation of television advertising costs during this period. Figure 4.2 presents data collected from the Television Bureau of Advertising that indicates that television advertising has become significantly more expensive across all categories between 1972 and 2012. The average cost to reach 1,000 households during primetime on network television has jumped from $10.77 in 1972 to $24.08 in 2012 (in real dollars). Similar increases can be observed for other advertising

TABLE 4.1 Average Campaign Expenditures U.S. House (1972–2018)

Election Year	Incumbents	Challengers	Successful Challengers
2018	1,812,685	1,202,705	5,652,285
2016	1,554,923	329,968	2,730,847
2014	1,557,737	442,874	2,226,359
2012	1,706,967	562,134	2,860,652
2010	1,779,103	693,887	1,866,073
2008	1,596,700	575,327	2,358,598
2006	1,607,782	545,338	2,291,668
2004	1,377,072	358,099	2,229,618
2002	1,255,312	354,796	2,195,084
2000	1,253,215	445,339	2,891,085
1998	1,001,746	399,144	1,769,428
1996	1,071,768	422,169	1,740,875
1994	935,743	354,057	1,120,570
1992	955,267	280,456	793,356
1990	780,299	209,316	836,118
1988	821,772	255,903	1,231,537
1986	803,861	293,859	1,207,201
1984	694,316	308,205	1,227,215
1982	646,853	314,530	748,537
1980	526,346	303,143	1,036,759
1978	466,296	276,359	835,770
1976	358,600	229,418	638,214
1974	301,452	204,059	511,217
1972	312,352	188,897	669,730

Spending (shaded on a log-scale) 13 14 15

All amounts adjusted for inflation (in 2018 real dollars)
(Data compiled by author from Jacobson Challenger Quality Measures)

categories, including spot and cable advertising rates per 1,000 households (see Figure 4.2).

Increasing rates of cable penetration (displayed in Figure 4.3) have made television advertising more accessible and affordable for congressional campaigns (as opposed to presidential campaigns that regularly invest in network advertising). Data presented in Figure 4.4 reveal that political campaigns increasingly rely on spot and local television advertisements. The data presented in Figure 4.2 show that cable advertising has also become more expensive over time. In 1982 (the earliest year for which data on cable data is available), the average cost to reach 1,000 households during primetime in the top 100 markets on cable was $8.87 ($21.10 in real 2012 dollars). By 2012, the cost to reach a similar audience had increased to $32.08 (in real dollars).

These developments in television advertising costs alone help support the claim that campaigns became more and more expensive between 1972 and 2018. Still

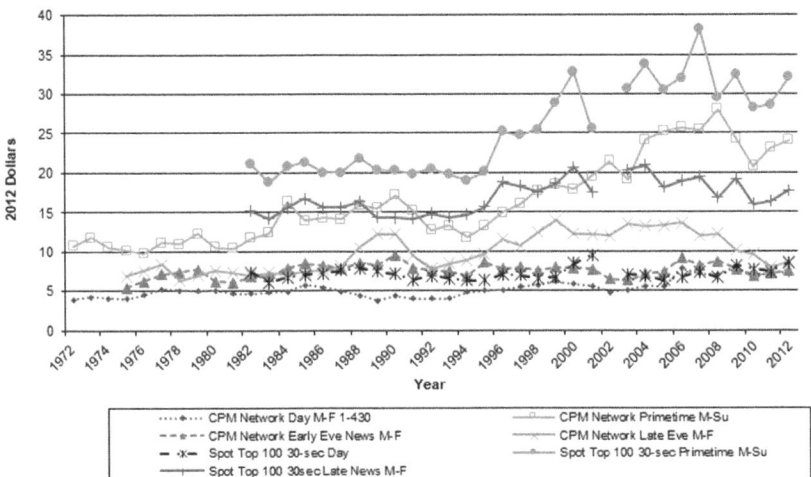

FIGURE 4.2 Average Television Advertising Costs (CPM) for Various Times, 1972–2012

other developments may contribute to escalating campaign costs. Other scholars argue that candidates rely less on the political parties for campaign services than they did in the past. Campaigns must increasingly purchase these costly services (polling, get-out-the-vote, research, media production) on their own (Thurber and Nelson 2000; Panagopoulos 2017). Beyond that, lower levels of campaign and party volunteers and increasing campaign execution professionalization means that campaigns must hire costly professionals to perform work previously done by volunteers.

Estimating campaign costs, and evaluating developments in campaign costs over several decades, is a tall task. Even the previous discussion about television advertising excludes any reflections on developments in radio, direct mail, other media, and forms of voter contact. Given that politicians must reach more people, more frequently, with more—and more expensive—media messages than in the past, it is a reasonable assertion that campaign costs rose between 1972 and 2018. The difficulty is compounded by the aim to estimate and compare campaign costs across districts over time. Thanks to the 1974 FECA legislation, we do, however, have reliable measures of campaign spending in districts during this period compiled by the Federal Election Commission. While campaign spending is not exactly a measure of campaign costs, campaign finance data can serve as a useful indicator of cost available at the district level[1] (Berkman 1994. Campaigns spend money because they feel they need to do so in order to win. For the purposes of this study, the most relevant point about campaign costs is the signal costs send to challengers or potential challengers. When they evaluate the political environment and assess both their prospects for victory and the resources required to

52 Money and Challenger Quality

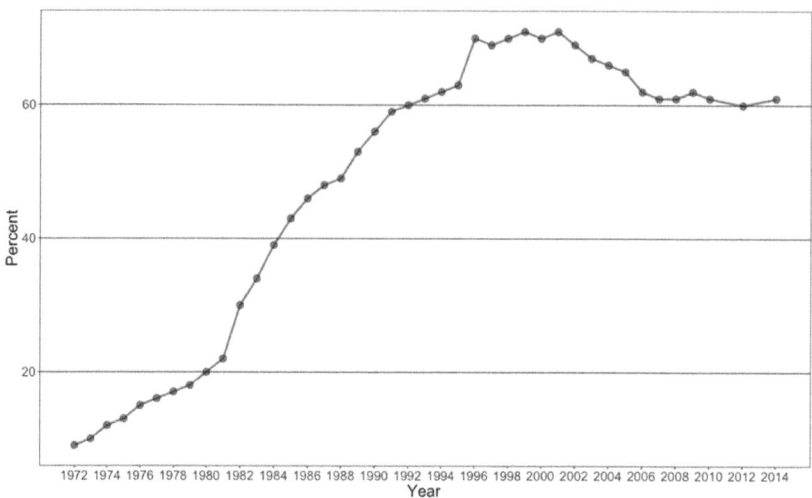

FIGURE 4.3 Cable TV Penetration, 1972–2014

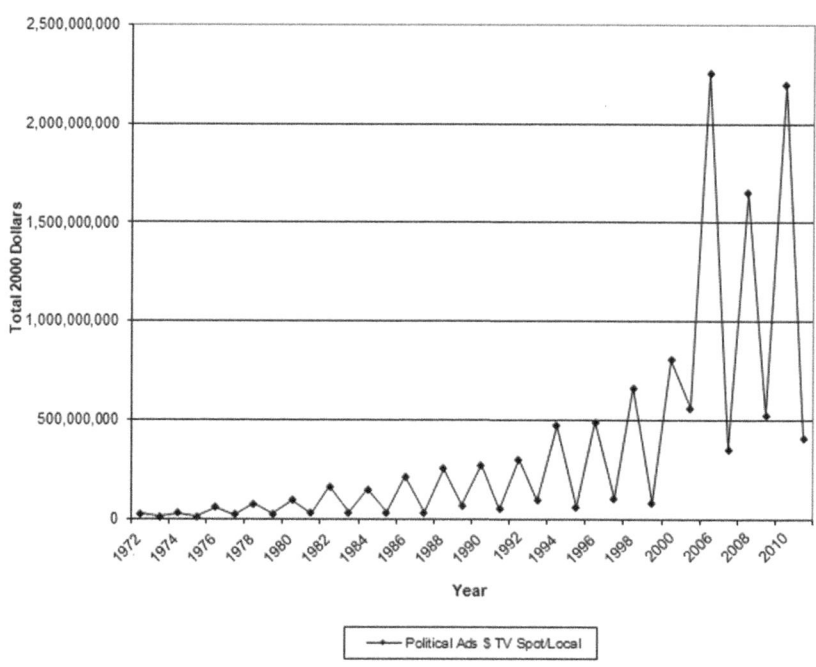

FIGURE 4.4 Total Spending on Political TV Advertising, Spot/Local, 1972–2014

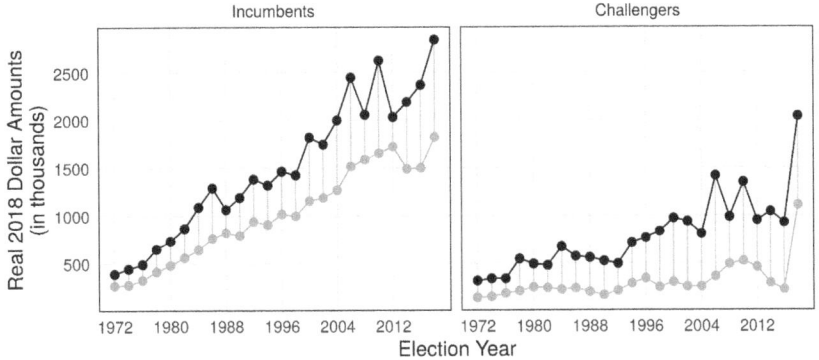

FIGURE 4.5 Average Campaign Expenditures by Candidate and Challenger Types (1972–2018)

achieve that goal, the best indicator challengers have available is spending in previous elections. For this reason, I consider campaign spending to be a reasonable measure of the cost of a campaign. By this metric, campaigns have clearly become more costly between 1972 and 2018.

Not only have campaigns become more expensive, but also challengers' access to funds has become increasingly limited. Researchers report that incumbents are systematically advantaged when it comes to financing campaigns (Brady et al. 2000). Figure 4.5 presents average campaign expenditures by candidate and challenger type for election cycles 1972–2018. Figures 4.1 and 4.5 both demonstrate that challengers are consistently outspent by incumbents. Figure 4.5 (left panel) shows that incumbents that run against high-quality challengers spend more, on average, than incumbents who run against low-quality challengers. (The data also show that high-quality challengers expend more on campaigns, on average, than low-quality challengers.) When average challenger spending is calculated as a proportion of average incumbent spending, challengers' expenditures have decreased significantly relative to their incumbent counterparts. The findings indicate that average challenger spending, as a function of average incumbent spending, has dropped by about 1.1% for each election cycle between 1972 and 2018 (Data not shown; OLS time series regression coefficient $=-1.11$; $t=-3.13$; $p<.01$; $N=24$).

One plausible explanation for incumbents' campaign funding advantage is the role played by political action committees. These groups have become key players in financing congressional campaigns since the 1970s, and their resources have been directed primarily toward incumbents. Consider that the number of PACs currently registered with the Federal Election Commission exceeds 3,000 and

54 Money and Challenger Quality

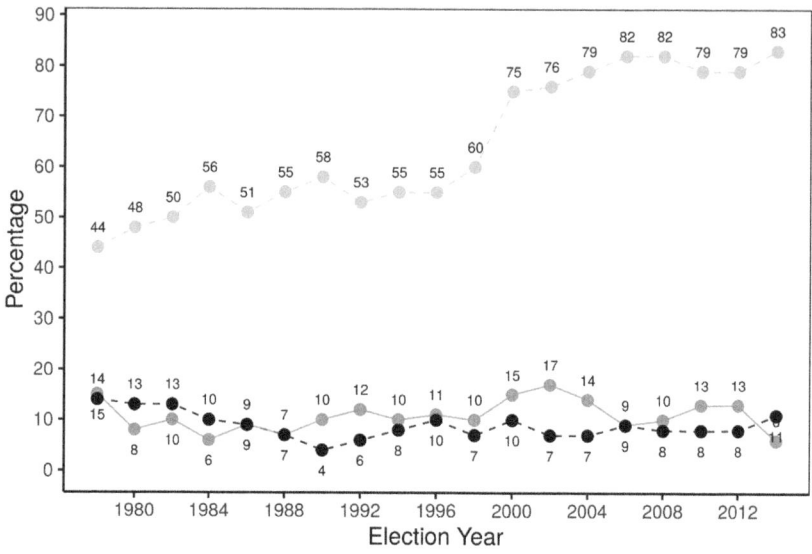

FIGURE 4.6 Proportion of Total PAC Contributions to U.S. House Candidates: Candidates by type (1978–2014)

that, on average, over half of the total PAC resources are distributed to incumbents seeking reelection. Figure 4.6 displays the proportion of total PAC contributions that is distributed to candidates for the U.S. House by type of candidate between 1978 and 2014. The data demonstrate that the proportion of total PAC money that has been directed toward House incumbents has steadily increased with each election cycle, reaching a peak of 83% in 2014. Challengers in U.S. House elections, on the other hand, consistently receive less than 15% of all PAC contributions during each election cycle. The data presented in Figure 4.6 reveal that challengers systematically have less access to campaign funding from political action committees. While there has been a significant increase between 1978 and 2014 in the proportion of PAC funds directed to incumbents (OLS time series regression shows a 1.15% increase on average for each cycle; $N = 19$; $t = 10.00$), the proportion dedicated to challengers has decreased by 0.08% per cycle ($N = 19$; $t = -2.02$, $p = 0.09$). (No statistically significant change for the proportion of PAC funds directed to open seat races.)

All of this amounts to a situation in which challengers find it more difficult to launch competitive campaigns. Figure 4.7 demonstrates that, on average, fewer than 7% of challengers raise enough funds in each election cycle to be competitive

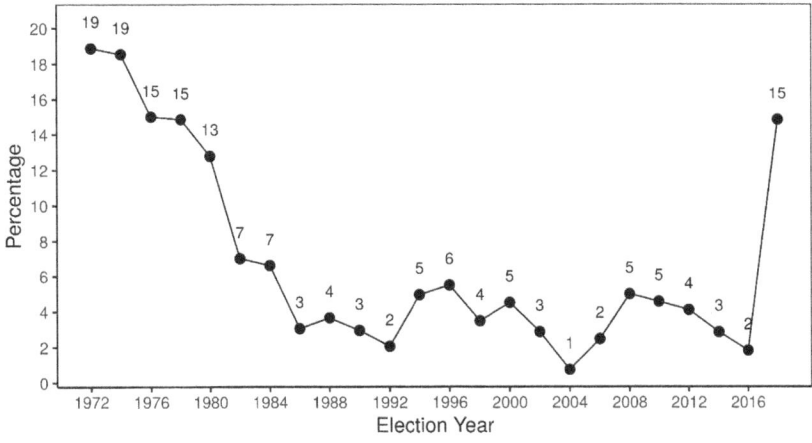

FIGURE 4.7 Proportion of Challengers with Competitive Expenditure Levels (1972–2018)

against their incumbent opponents. (A challenger is defined to be competitive when their expenditure level equals or exceeds their incumbent opponent.) In no election cycle since 1972 have more than two out of ten challengers overall matched or exceeded the expenditure levels of incumbents in the same cycle. In the five most recent elections, less than 6% of challengers have waged financially competitive campaigns against incumbents on average (with the main exception of 2018, an especially competitive year). In fact, the findings show that since 1972, the proportion of challengers who were able to match or exceed the expenditure levels of their opponents has systematically declined by almost 0.5% in each election cycle (OLS time series regression coefficient = −0.463; t = −3.370, N = 24).

Challengers overall are increasingly less competitive financially. Generally, this finding holds for both high-quality challengers and low-quality challengers. Figure 4.8 breaks down the proportion of challengers who either met or exceeded their opponents' spending amounts by the quality of the challenger. The results indicate that, typically, a greater proportion of high-quality challengers are competitive than low-quality challengers in any given election cycle. On average, the proportion of competitive high-quality challengers is almost twice that of low-quality challengers (13% compared to 7% respectively) between 1972 and 2018. Yet the proportions of both categories of challengers have experienced statistically significant decline. An OLS time series analysis (the estimated slope of the coefficient from a regression of the dependent variable on a constant and a time trend) shows that the proportion of competitive high-quality challengers has dropped by about one percentage point for each cycle (OLS time series coefficient = −0.83; t = −3.73, p < 0.01) and the proportion of competitive low-quality challengers

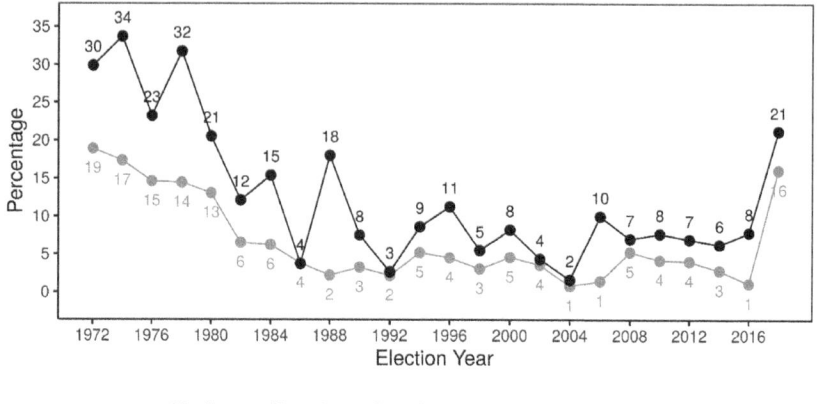

FIGURE 4.8 Proportion of Challengers with Competitive Expenditure Levels by Type (1972–2018)

by nearly 0.5 percentage points (OLS time series coefficient=−0.44; t=−3.12, p<0.01). In fact, this analysis shows that the decline in competitiveness of high-quality challengers has declined more sharply than low-quality challengers. The key result, however, is that the overall decline in the proportion of competitive challengers is not a phenomenon driven by either high or low-quality challengers. Both categories of challengers are contributing to the overall decrease.

Readers may argue that defining "competitiveness" as such is too harsh. A more reasonable approach may be to consider challengers who spend, say, at least half as much as their incumbent opponents as "competitive." Figure 4.9 displays the proportion of challengers with competitive expenditure levels at varying levels of "competitiveness" for election cycles 1972–2018. The findings indicate that, even if we relax the criteria and define challengers to be "competitive" when they spend as little as 50% as much as their opponents, less than a quarter of all challengers between 1972 and 2018 (21%) spent "competitive" amounts in their campaigns. (Figure 4.9 also indicates the proportion of challengers who spent at least two-thirds as much as their opponents.) Moreover, the proportion of challengers who can be defined as "competitive" at the 50% level has also systematically declined by nearly one percentage point in each cycle during this period (OLS time series regression coefficient=−0.91; t=−4.52; N=24, p<0.001).

Summary

This chapter describes key developments in financing congressional campaigns and campaign costs since the 1970s. These developments can plausibly influence challenger quality in congressional elections. In the chapters that follow, we

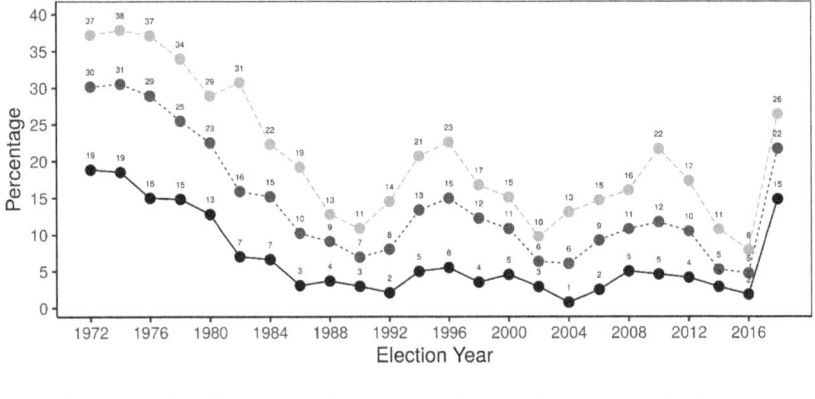

FIGURE 4.9 Proportion of Challengers with Competitive Expenditure Levels (at Various Levels) (1972–2018)

will examine the impact of campaign costs and campaign spending on candidate emergence in elections for Congress.

Note

1 To illustrate the point, consider that the Pearson's correlation between total aggregate campaign spending and average CPM for a 30-second television ad broadcast during primetime is 0.95.

5
CANDIDATE QUALITY AND CAMPAIGN COMMUNICATIONS STRATEGIES

Most of the discussion surrounding the differences between high and low-quality candidates focuses on electoral outcomes. As I discuss in previous chapters, Jacobson (1990) noted that experienced challengers are four times as likely as inexperienced challengers to defeat incumbents (Jacobson 1990), an effect that remains strong and robust over time. But what accounts for this phenomenon? There appear to exist some fundamental differences between high and low-quality candidates, yet their exact nature remains elusive. In order to productively examine the sources and consequences of candidate quality, we must also come to understand *why* these differences materialize. This chapter represents a bit of a digression to undertake an exploratory analysis that may help to address this question.

One explanation often asserted in the literature on congressional elections to explain experienced challengers' stronger electoral performance is campaign aptitude. Scholars commonly claim that challengers with prior elective experience possess superior campaigning abilities (Cox and Katz 2002; Herrnson 1995; Canon 1990; Jacobson 1990). Politicians with previously successful electoral experience simply make better strategic decisions about campaign execution and strategy. Despite how widespread this belief is in the literature, it has received limited scholarly attention. Herrnson (2004) observes some key differences in communications strategies between various candidate categories, but he devises an alternative measure of candidate quality and relies on survey responses for his analysis. This chapter aims to extend this work by examining empirical evidence from campaign messages actually broadcast on television by candidates' campaigns to test whether or not there are differences in communications strategies between incumbents, experienced, and inexperienced candidates for Congress.

Prior experience, access to resources and information, and familiarity with districts all permit incumbents to make better decisions than challengers about campaign communications strategies. Among challengers, politically experienced challengers should theoretically make better campaign communications decisions than politically inexperienced challengers. The first hypothesis that emerges from these assertions is that we should observe differences in campaign communications strategies between experienced and inexperienced challengers. Second, we may also hypothesize that experienced challengers' campaign communications strategy decisions should resemble incumbents' choices more so than inexperienced challengers' communications decisions. This chapter will test these two hypotheses by analyzing the tone, style, and content of political television advertisements broadcast by candidates during the 1998 congressional elections.

Television advertisements are currently the predominant communications medium for candidates for the U.S. Congress (Panagopoulos 2017). Darrell West (1994) claims that commercials have become the major strategic tool for contesting elections in America and finds that candidates devote the largest proportion of their overall campaign budgets to advertising. Roughly nine in ten Senate candidates and 65% of all House campaigns produce and air television ads (Herrnson 1995). The typical candidate directs the lion's share of their campaign budget to television advertising (West 1994; Panagopoulos 2017). Television ads are also effective at informing voters. West's study finds that voters learn more about issues from advertisements than from the news (West 1994). He also finds that ads influence how voters learn about candidates, what they identify as priorities, what standards voters use to assess candidates, and how voters attribute blame (West 1994). These findings suggest that it would not be an overstatement to view television political advertisements as the primary communications vehicle in congressional campaigns. In fact, Herrnson (1995: 214) argues that television is the "best medium for conveying image-related information to a mass audience [and is] ... extremely useful in setting the campaign agenda and associating a candidate with popular issues."

The data used for the analyses in this chapter comes from a database of political advertising broadcast in 1998 that was collected by the Campaign Media Analysis Group (CMAG). CMAG, a firm that specializes in advising political clients, uses satellite technology originally developed for the U.S. Navy to track Soviet submarines to monitor the transmission of political advertisements aired in the top 75 (of 216) media markets across the nation. This technology makes an unprecedented amount of data about political advertisements available for research. The system monitored broadcasts from national networks (ABC, CBS, NBC, and FOX), 25 national cable networks (CNN, ESPN, TBS) and local advertising in the country's top markets. In total, these markets included over 80% of the U.S. population in 1998.

CMAG's software recognizes the electronic seams between programming and advertising. When the system first detects a commercial spot's unique sound pattern, it downloads the ad and creates a storyboard (the full audio and every four seconds of video). (CMAG also adds information about the date, time, and station on which the ad appeared as well as the estimated cost of the commercial.) These storyboards enable a research team at the University of Wisconsin to undertake an extensive coding exercise that adds additional information about the style and content of each ad.

In 1998, CMAG tracked over 2,100 separate ads aired over 300,000 times by or on behalf of political candidates running for federal office. Only ads for federal candidates were included in the database. The data set includes ads from 194 House and Senate races. (Although there were certainly many more than 194 races taking place across the country, many congressional candidates either opted not to advertise on television or found it cost effective to allocate resources to alternative forms of communication—such as direct mail—when, for example, district and media market boundaries did not overlap closely. These cases are excluded from the sample.)

The CMAG database contained a substantial amount of information about each political ad that was broadcast in 1998. Details include whether the candidate favored in the ad is a Democrat or a Republican, who sponsored the ad (candidate, party, or other group) and whether the ad was a candidate ad or an issue ad. However, the database is organized at the individual ad level and not at the candidate level. Thus, using variables that indicated the favored candidate in the ad, the state and congressional district of the race, and the party of the featured candidate, it was necessary to recode the data to organize it at the candidate level. I also coded the quality of the challenger for each ad broadcast by a challenger as well as the quality of the challenging opponent for each ad broadcast by an incumbent.

I include contested U.S. House races against incumbents in my analysis. I excluded issue ads and consider only candidate ads that were sponsored by candidates. My rationale for this decision was that candidate-sponsored ads would best represent communications strategy decisions made exclusively by candidates and their organizations. In addition, I only considered ads that were broadcast in general election contests. Incumbent candidates broadcast 66% of all ads (40,920 airings total). Of the challengers' 21,263 ad airings, 45% (9,497) were broadcast by experienced challengers while 55% (11,766) were aired by inexperienced challengers. My sample includes the entire universe of campaigns that broadcast political advertising on television during the general election cycle. This study uses each ad *airing* as the unit of analysis. (See Prior (2001) and Goldstein and Freedman (2000) for a detailed discussion about why it is best to study actual ads aired in a given market rather than ads produced overall.)

To look for differences by candidate status, I examined the tone, style, and policy content of the ads in the dataset. To determine the tone of the ad, I considered whether the ad was coded as an ad whose purpose was to promote, attack, or contrast. For style, I examined the kinds of adjectives candidates used in their ads either to describe themselves or their opponent. To examine content, I considered several questions that coded each ad's campaign theme. Each ad was coded so as to denote whether its general focus was personal or policy-related. Then, content was coded for the specific campaign theme or policy issue. (I rely on content coding conducted by the research team at the University of Wisconsin. For details about coding procedures, see Krasno and Seltz 2000.)

I conduct difference of means tests (t-tests) to analyze differences in candidates' advertising decisions across candidate types. Analysis of the t-test results produces some initial insights about the relationship between candidate quality and campaign communications strategies.

Findings: Comparison of Means

Figure 5.1 displays the findings of the comparison of means by candidate status. Bars in each row indicate the percent of total ads aired by candidates of similar status that were characterized by the specific attribute. Difference of means statistics (t-test) reveal that all differences across categories for all attributes are significant at conventional levels ($p < 0.05$) unless otherwise indicated.

Figure 5.1 reveals that the tone of ads does vary by candidate status, as shown by the color of bars. Incumbents broadcast primarily promotional ads (67% of total, versus 11% attack ads and 19% contrast ads). Only 43% of experienced challenger's ads are promotional, however (19% are attack ads and 33% are contrast). Inexperienced challengers run equal shares of promotional and attack ads (35% of total each), however, relative to high-quality challengers, inexperienced challengers broadcast a smaller share of promotional ads and a substantially larger share of attack ads against incumbents than high-quality challengers do.

Figure 5.1 also examines the styles employed by different candidate types in campaign ads. Each ad was evaluated to determine whether candidates used certain adjectives to describe themselves or their opponent in the ads. Figure 5.1 reveals that incumbents portray themselves as "honest" in 3% of their ads, while 2% of experienced challengers' ads present the candidate as honest, and a negligible percent of inexperienced challengers' ads do the same. A greater proportion of incumbents' ads describe them as "competent" (7% of total), while 5% of experienced challengers' ads and 1% of inexperienced challengers' ads use this adjective. Nearly one-tenth (9%) of inexperienced challengers' ads portray them as "protectors," compared to 4% of incumbents' ads and 6% of experienced challengers' ads. Over one-in-five (21%) experienced challengers' ads characterize them as "tough" (20% of incumbents' ads do the same) compared with only one-in-ten inexperienced challengers' ads.

Figure 5.1 also indicates differences in adjectives candidates use to describe opponents by candidate type. Fewer incumbent ads characterize challengers as "dishonest or corrupt" (7%), compared to 11% of high-quality challengers' ads and 16% of low-quality challengers' ads. Incumbents also describe challengers as "taxing" substantially less frequently (3% of all incumbent ads) than inexperienced

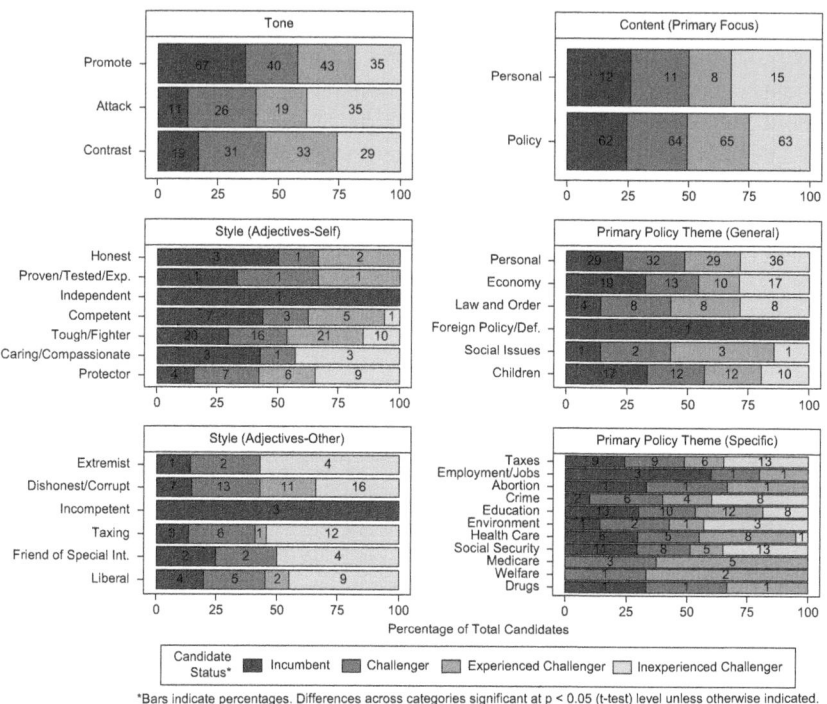

FIGURE 5.1 Comparison of Means by Candidate Status for each Ad Attribute

challengers (12%) (1% of experienced challengers' ads present incumbents as "taxing"). Inexperienced challengers also describe their opponents as "friends of special interests" (4%) and "liberal" (9%) more often than experienced incumbents. By contrast, incumbents characterize their opponents as "incompetent" in 3% of their ads, while neither category of challengers appears to describe incumbents as such.

Moving on to the substance of ad content, Figure 5.1 shows that most of all candidates' ads focus on policy matters rather than personal characteristics (62% of incumbents' ads, 65% of experienced challengers, and 63% of inexperienced challengers' ads.) Inexperienced challengers run far more ads that focus on personal qualities (15% of total) compared to experienced challengers (8%). Twelve percent of incumbents' ads focus on personal characteristics.

To examine the general campaign theme candidates emphasized in their ads, I divided each specific policy into six categories. Figure 5.1 shows the proportions of primary campaign themes across categories of candidates. Candidates coded with a focus on personal characteristics broadcast ads whose primary campaign theme was one of the following: Candidate background, political record, attendance record, ideology, personal values, honesty/integrity, or special interests. Ads were categorized as economy if they included either of the following themes: Taxes, deficit/budget/surplus/debt, government spending, minimum wage, farming, business, employment/jobs, poverty, or trade. Social issues include abortion, homosexuality, moral values, tobacco, affirmative action, gambling, assisted suicide, or gun control. Law and order themes include crime, drugs, or the death penalty. Children's issues include education, lottery for education, and child-care. Foreign policy/defense theme incorporates defense, missile defense, veterans, foreign policy, Bosnia, or China. Additional themes are considered separately.

Figure 5.1 shows that all types of candidates' ads whose theme was policy focused heavily on the economy, children, and law and order. The data indicate that inexperienced challengers' ads targeted the economy far more than experienced challengers' ads (17% versus 10%, respectively). Nineteen percent of incumbents' ads focused on the economy as a policy issue. Experienced challengers discussed children's issues in their ads more so than low-quality challengers (12% versus 10%, respectively). Differences between inexperienced and experienced challengers are muted with respect to issues of law and order and foreign policy/defense. Incumbents and inexperienced challengers emphasize social issues in 1% of their ads, while experienced challengers address this issue in 3% of their ads.

To probe campaign themes further, Figure 5.1 shows differences between types of contenders for Congress by specific policy area. Incumbents run a greater share of ads about jobs (3%) and education (13%) than both experienced (1% and 12%, respectively) and inexperienced challengers (0% and 8%, respectively). Inexperienced challengers discuss taxes, crime, the environment, and social security more frequently than both incumbents and experienced challengers. High-quality challengers discuss education, jobs, abortion, health care, Medicare, welfare, and drugs more often than inexperienced challengers did in the 1998 elections.

Challenger Quality and Incumbent Communication Strategy

In this section, I examine differences between candidates' communications strategies from another perspective. I analyze data presented in Figure 5.2 to determine whether or not incumbents communicate differently with voters when their opponents are experienced challengers rather than when their opponents lack prior elective experience. In 1998, incumbent candidates aired

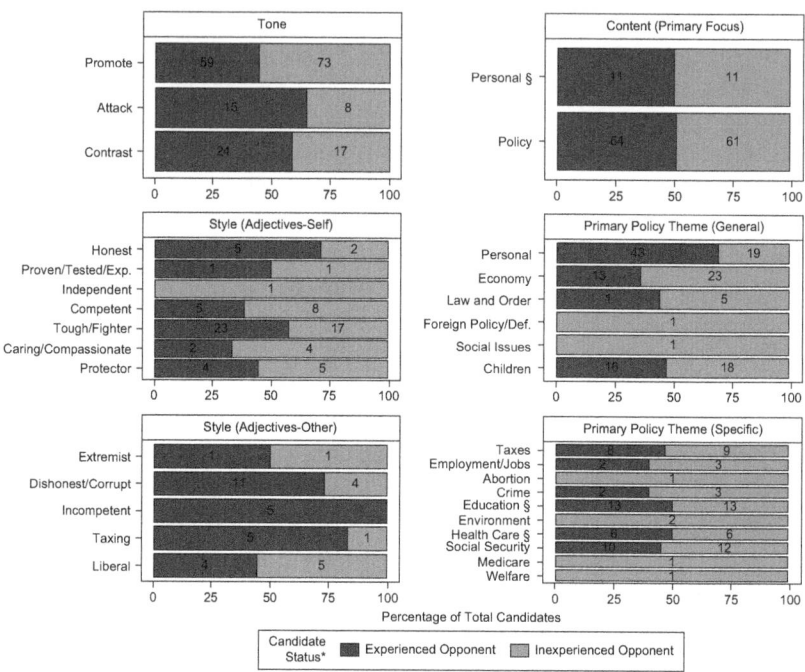

FIGURE 5.2 Incumbents' Communication Strategies by Opponent Type

a total of 16,134 ads when running against high-quality challengers and a total of 24,786 ads in races against low-quality challengers. These are the base sample sizes for the analyses presented in Figure 5.2, and the proportions indicated in them are based on these. The findings demonstrate some clear differences in strategy that depend on the quality of the opponent. The data presented in Figure 5.2 suggest that incumbents treat inexperienced challengers with kid gloves in their television advertisements, at least relative to the tone they adopt in their campaign communications against experienced opponents. Nearly three in four (73%) of incumbents' ad airings are positive in tone when facing low-quality opposition compared to 59% of their ads when running against electorally experienced opponents. Incumbents also tend to attack experienced challengers more often than inexperienced opponents. Fifteen percent of all incumbents' ads were attack ads when they ran against high-quality challengers, versus 8% of incumbents' ads when they run against challengers with no prior elective experience. Incumbents present themselves as "honest" and "tough" more often when running against experienced colleagues (5% and

23%, respectively) than inexperienced challengers (2% and 17%, respectively). Incumbents characterize experienced opponents as "dishonest/corrupt," "incompetent," and "taxing" (11%, 5%, and 5%, respectively) more regularly than inexperienced contenders (4%, 0%, 1%, respectively). Incumbents portray inexperienced challengers as "liberal" (5%) slightly more often than experienced challengers (4%).

Challenger quality also seems to play a role in the decisions incumbent candidates make about policy content in their ads depending on whether they face a high or low-quality challenger at the polls. Incumbents run a greater share of ads about policy when they run against experienced challengers (64% versus 61%, respectively). Incumbents broadcast a substantially larger share of ads about the economy when facing an inexperienced challenger (23% versus 13%). The differences are smaller with respect to the other general policy themes. As a general advertising theme, incumbents devote a larger share of ads (43%) to personal characteristics when running against high-quality challengers compared with low-quality challengers (19%). I also observe a greater emphasis on taxes, jobs, environment, abortion, crime, social security, Medicare, and welfare when incumbents run against inexperienced opponents, but challenger quality does not appear to influence focus on education or health care issues.

Results

The analyses above reveal a variety of systematic differences in campaign communications strategies by candidate types with respect to decisions about specific features of campaign communications. To what extent, however, do the findings provide support for the two hypotheses that motivate this analysis? Specifically, do we observe systematic differences in communications strategies overall between experienced and inexperienced challengers? And, do experienced challengers overall behave more like incumbents than inexperienced challengers do?

The average difference between the overall proportion of ads with each of the individual attributes described above between experienced and inexperienced challengers is 4.11 percentage points (standard error = 3.7). Thus, the average difference in overall communications strategy decisions is slightly more than four percentage points. The Pearson's R correlation coefficient between the overall communications strategy decisions of experienced and inexperienced challengers is 0.92 (significant at $p < 0.01$). This evidence suggests that while there may be systematic differences in campaign communications strategies between high and low-quality challengers, these differences, although statistically significant, are, on the whole, rather small. Based on my assessment of the results, I conclude that we observe limited differences between challenger types between high and low-quality challengers. In fact, we observe remarkable similarity in overall campaign communications strategies.

To the extent that we observe differences in campaign communications strategies between experienced and inexperienced challengers, do experienced challengers' decisions resemble incumbents' decisions more so than inexperienced challengers' communications strategy decisions do? The average difference between incumbents' communications strategy decisions and experienced challengers is 3.27 percentage points (standard error = 4.5). Experienced challengers' campaign communications decisions correlate with incumbents' choice at 0.93 (Pearson's R correlation coefficient significant at $p < 0.01$). The average difference between inexperienced challengers' communications choices and incumbents' decisions is 4.78 percentage points (standard error = 6.4). The Pearson's R correlation coefficient between inexperienced challengers' strategy decisions and incumbents' is 0.85 (significant at $p < 0.01$). These findings confirm that experienced challengers' overall campaign communications strategies do resemble incumbents' overall strategies more so than inexperienced challengers' strategies do. Yet these analyses reflect more similarities between challenger types than differences. Even as inexperienced challengers communicate slightly differently with constituents than experienced challengers, at least in terms of the contents of advertisements broadcasted on television, these differences are not sizeable. Moreover, we observe considerable resemblance in communication strategies between inexperienced challengers' choices and incumbent behavior, even as this correspondence is somewhat greater for high-quality challengers.

Conclusions

The results of this analysis suggest we should be cautious about attributing the stronger electoral performance of experienced challengers to superior campaigning ability. At least with respect to televisions advertising, the strategic choices of experienced challengers do not differ dramatically from inexperienced challengers' decisions. Moreover, while we observe statistically significant differences in campaign communications strategies by candidate types, these differences are typically not large. As a whole, incumbents do not seem to behave very differently from either experienced or inexperienced challengers. In other words, candidate status seems to matter in campaign communications strategies but not always for very much.

These results create a different perspective on the study of challenger quality and incumbency advantage. The majority of work on the differences between experienced and inexperienced candidates has focused on electoral outcomes. Collaterally, it is easy to assume that these outcomes occur because of fundamental differences between the candidates. This analysis, although limited in scope, raises doubts about this assumption. It indicates that there may not be a substantial difference between the communication styles (and, in turn, campaign strategies) of candidates with and without political experience.

6

MOVIN' ON UP

The Impact of State Legislative Term Limits on Candidate Quality in U.S. House Elections, 1972–2018

Frustration with soaring incumbency advantage, near-maximum levels of incumbent reelection rates and the danger of diminished responsiveness from elected officials fueled the state legislative term limits movement in the 1980s and early 1990s (Farmer, Rausch and Green 2003). Limiting tenure became the solution many reformers advocated to dissolve what Gary Jacobson has called the "ossified ruling clique," out of touch with voters and responsive only to special interests (Jacobson 2001: 276). Enhanced electoral competition, thus, was one of the primary aims that state legislative term limits were intended to achieve (Grofman 1996; Farmer, Rausch, and Green 2003).

From an academic perspective, investigating the expectation that state legislative term limits would increase electoral competition became the focus of much scholarly pursuit in the field (Farmer et al. 2003; Petracca 1996). Researchers who examine this topic are guided partly by ambition theory, initially developed and applied to electoral politics by Schlesigner (1966). Schlesigner believed that "ambition lies at the heart of politics, and that politics thrive on the hope of preferment and the drive for office" (1966: 1). Broadly conceptualized, ambition theory posits that politicians' actions are driven by their prospective political ambition. Schlesigner distinguished between three forms of ambition: discrete (those who aim to attain a specific office for a limited, temporary period), static (those who aim to attain a specific office for the long term), and progressive (those who constantly seek upward moves to higher elective positions (Schlesigner 1966; Farmer et al. 2003).

Subsequent research refined Schlesigner's notion of ambition theory. Black (1972) and Rhode (1979) modified the theory to cast it in utility maximizing form (Aldrich 1995). In these reformulations, which represent a partial departure from Schlesigner's original argument, all incumbents are assumed to prefer holding a higher office to a lower office and all prefer holding office to holding no office at all (Aldrich 1995). The implications of ambition theory for the study of the impact of state legislative term limits are readily clear. It is reasonable to expect that term limited officials will seek other electoral opportunities, perhaps especially, but not exclusively, for higher office.

While this expectation may be reasonable, it is more problematic to establish a clear hierarchy of elective positions. Is a county-level seat, for example, a move upwards for a state legislator or is a local seat in a large city a move downward? It is challenging to test this theory empirically in a system with so little rigidity.

Nevertheless, some studies provide preliminary evidence from states that have implemented state legislative term limits. In his study of the career paths of 180 term-limited state legislators in the six states with active limits in 1998, Powell (2003) finds that nearly half (44%) of the outgoing state legislators chose not to run for subsequent office. Of the 97 who did run for office again, the vast majority (65%) ran for state-level offices, 29% ran for local or county-level positions and only six state legislators ran for federal office (in Farmer et al. 2003). Powell's study also shows that a sizeable proportion of term-limited members (29%) move on to non-elective political positions, but that the greatest share (44%) exit the political arena entirely (Farmer et al. 2003).

Contrary to the predictions of ambition theory, Powell's study demonstrates that many term-limited state legislators do not seek further office. Amongst those who do, it is unclear that all (or even most) seek "higher" office. While, in theory, state legislative term limits should augment electoral competition, the empirical analysis yields uncertain conclusions. Similarly, related research offers mixed conclusions about the effectiveness of state legislative term limits in generating higher levels of electoral competition. Case studies revealed no appreciable change in the levels of electoral competition in Colorado and Maine, for example, and only minimal change in Michigan. A more substantial increase in the number of candidates was, however, observed in California (Farmer et al. 2003). Powell (2000) has demonstrated that state legislators in term-limited states are more likely to run for the U.S. House. Similarly, Francis and Kenney (1997) have shown that state house members are more likely to run for state senate in states with state legislative term limits. For the most part, however, the findings remain inconclusive and preliminary, and additional research is necessary.

This chapter examines the impact of state legislative term limits on electoral competition in races for the U.S. House of Representatives. I will test several hypotheses to probe whether the introduction of state legislative term limits has affected overall levels of electoral competition in U.S. House races at the aggregate level. I will also analyze how state legislative term limits are impacting electoral competition for U.S. House seats in states that have already implemented limits.

The introduction of state legislative term limits in some states (but not others) creates a quasi-natural experiment ripe for social scientific inquiry. This study is structured to take advantage of the benefits of a quasi-experimental design, seeking to compare effects in the treatment group (term-limited states) to the control group (all other states). I will also consider the effect of state legislative term limits *within* states that have implemented limits by comparing candidate quality levels over time.

Most of the literature suggests that state legislative term limits will have a *direct* effect on US House race competition. As term-limited state legislators are forced out of office, they are likely to run for higher seats, including U.S. House seats. There is also the possibility that state legislative term limits affect electoral competition for U.S. House seats *indirectly*. The presence of state legislative term limits for state legislative seats may discourage other elected officials (i.e., those elected to positions other than state legislative seats) from seeking positions in the state legislature. Rather than compete for seats in the state legislature, which they will—at best—possess only temporarily because these are affected by state legislative term limits, these elected officials may opt to run for Congress instead. Either way, the expectation is that state legislative term limits will increase the levels of electoral competition in U.S. House races. I hypothesize that *increases in the prevalence of active state legislative term limits will increase electoral competition in U.S. House races.*

Data and Measurement

One way to measure electoral competition in U.S. House races is to consider the level of *challenger quality* in these contests. The theoretical literature suggests that strong challengers do not emerge randomly and that their occurrence varies with the prospects of victory (Jacobson 1989). Politicians—behaving as rational actors—will be "strategic" in their decision to run against incumbents and will opt to challenge incumbents when conditions make incumbents most vulnerable (Jacobson and Kernell 1981; Jacobson 1989; Maisel et al. 2001). By and large, high-quality challengers prefer to wait for an open seat in which there is no incumbent with their requisite advantages (Jacobson and Kernell 1981; Banks and Kiewiet 1989).

State legislative term limits, however, may alter the strategic calculations of potential challengers. Term-limited state legislators—who are, by definition, high-quality according to Jacobson—may not have the option to remain in the state-level positions as they wait for an open seat to become available. Consequently, many may choose to challenge incumbents. This should increase the overall level of challenger quality, in the aggregate. Moreover, state legislative term limits are also likely to increase the overall quality of candidates in open seats across the country. This section will investigate these expectations.

In Chapter 1, I show that the aggregate proportion of high-quality challengers has systematically *declined* between 1972 and 2018. Do state legislative term limits affect the overall level of challenger quality in U.S. House elections during this period? While some factors may be driving the decline we observe in challenger quality during this period, state legislative term limits should be tugging in the opposite direction. In the chapters that follow, I will address this matter further. I will consider state legislative term limits as one variable in multivariate analyses to test for its effect on aggregate quality levels and well as in the individual-level analysis.

To begin this investigation, however, we can conduct some preliminary analyses and examine the dynamics of overall challenger quality in each state that has enacted state legislative term limits. By looking at changes within each state, over time, we can examine whether the introduction of state legislative term limits substantially alters the proportion of high-quality challengers within the state. Table 6.1 reveals the results of an analysis of the proportion of experienced challengers in contested House races. "Limits in Place" represents House races during the period when state limits were in force, while "No Limits" represents races during periods when state limits had not yet been enacted or had been repealed. The initial findings suggest that state legislative term limits may not exert a positive effect on the proportion of high-quality challengers in races against incumbent members of the U.S. House. In 38% (8/21) of the cases, the mean level of high-quality challengers increases after the implementation of limits. This effect, however, appears not to be large. On average, the introduction of state legislative

TABLE 6.1 Mean Levels of Aggregate Challenger Quality Given Limits in Place vs. No Limits by State (1972–2018)

	No Limits	Limits in Place	Change	Probability (p-value)
Arizona	13	17	+4	0.58
Arkansas	15	52	+37	0**
California	12	10	-2	0.37
Colorado	40	35	-5	0.6
Florida	12	16	+4	0.31
Idaho	48	0	-48	0.01*
Louisiana	13	38	+25	0.13
Maine	59	62	+3	0.85
Massachusetts	16	13	-3	0.79
Michigan	21	18	-3	0.43
Missouri	26	19	-8	0.22
Montana	45	43	-2	0.92
Nebraska	21	30	+9	0.45
Nevada	46	36	-11	0.51
Ohio	24	18	-6	0.15
Oklahoma	25	11	-14	0.13
Oregon	23	22	-1	0.94
South Dakota	46	38	-9	0.7
Utah	36	18	-18	0.25
Washington	22	28	+6	0.52
Wyoming	14	17	+2	0.89

Note: No limits represents races at which point state limits had not been enacted or had been repealed.
(Data compiled by author from Jacobson Challenger Quality Measures)

term limits actually *decreases* the proportion of high-quality challengers by almost 3% (3.42). More technically, the data reported in Table 6.1 indicate that only one statistically significant increase in the difference of means before and after limits was in effect in Arkansas ($p < 0.01$).

When states are divided into those with limits in effect and those without for the election cycles between 1996 and 2018 in which some states had limits in place, few differences emerge (except for 1996 when only two states had state legislative term limits, including California, which may present an inaccurate portrait of true effects) (see Table 6.2).

Increases in challenger quality can be achieved by term-limited legislators deciding to challenge incumbents at other levels of government (direct) or by other elected officials choosing to seek to unseat incumbents rather than run for state legislature (indirect). Either or both of these mechanisms may account for the results we find in the analysis of the dynamics of challenger quality conducted above. To consider the direct effect of state legislative term limits more explicitly, we may want to consider only the career decisions of state legislative members

TABLE 6.2 Mean Levels of Aggregate Challenger Quality by States with Limits vs. States without Limits (1996–2018)

	United States	No Limits	Limits in Place	Probability (p-value)
1996	20	21	13	0.09.
1998	24	25	22	0.59
2000	22	22	20	0.68
2002	15	16	14	0.68
2004	19	21	14	0.13
2006	17	19	15	0.35
2008	17	15	19	0.46
2010	21	19	25	0.24
2012	22	21	25	0.53
2014	20	22	18	0.46
2016	16	16	15	0.72
2018	10	9	12	0.35

Note: No limits represents races at which point state limits had not been enacted or had been repealed.
(Data compiled by author from Jacobson Challenger Quality Measures)

TABLE 6.3 Proportion of Challengers who were Previously State Legislators Given Limits in Places vs. No Limits By State (1972–2018)

	No Limits	Limits in Place	Change	Probability (p-value)
Arizona	5	7	+2	0.58
Arkansas	5	16	+11	0.12
California	2	2	+1	0.42
Colorado	28	23	-5	0.53
Florida	2	6	+4	0.05*
Idaho	39	0	-39	0.03*
Louisiana	2	12	+11	0.01**
Maine	53	48	-5	0.74
Massachusetts	5	11	+6	0.27
Michigan	10	8	-2	0.62
Missouri	14	11	-2	0.62
Montana	30	29	-1	0.94
Nebraska	10	10	0	0.95
Nevada	21	29	+8	0.57
Ohio	6	5	-1	0.73
Oklahoma	15	3	-12	0.07.
Oregon	11	17	+5	0.5
South Dakota	31	38	+7	0.75
Utah	17	8	-9	0.46
Washington	9	23	+14	0.03*
Wyoming	7	17	+10	0.52

Note: No limits represents races at which point state limits had not been enacted or had been repealed.
(Data compiled by author from Jacobson Challenger Quality Measures)

before and after state legislative term limits. The analysis presented in Table 6.3 reveals that in more than 52% of cases (11/21), the proportion of state legislators that challenged incumbents after limits were introduced increased. In 9/21 cases the proportion after limits dropped (in one case, there was no change before and after limits.) Although there are a lot of unanswered questions about the effects of term-limited legislators, it is important to note that the majority of significant differences before and after limits (3/5) were *increases* in the proportion of high-quality challengers or challengers who were state legislators. These findings lend some support to the argument that term-limited legislators will seek to unseat incumbents, thereby increasing electoral competition in U.S. House races against incumbents.

State Legislative Term Limits and Candidate Quality in Open Seat Races

The analyses above offer some evidence in support of the proposition that electoral competition for U.S. House races is enhanced by state legislative term limits when we consider only races that involve incumbents. Do state legislative term limits have a similar effect in open seat races for the U.S. House of Representatives?

TABLE 6.4 Proportion of Open Seat Races with At Least One High-Quality Candidate, Given Limits in Places vs. No Limits By State (1972–2018)

	No Limits	Limits in Place	Change	Probability (p-value)
Arizona	70	73	+3	0.86
Arkansas	83	67	-17	0.42
California	89	82	-6	0.36
Colorado	92	100	+8	0.35
Florida	78	67	-11	0.29
Idaho	86	100	+14	0.57
Louisiana	40	0	-40	0.09.
Maine	100	100	0	---
Massachusetts	79	100	+21	0.61
Michigan	74	76	+2	0.86
Missouri	86	75	-11	0.53
Montana	100	100	0	---
Nebraska	89	100	+11	0.73
Nevada	88	60	-28	0.25
Ohio	100	81	-19	0.03*
Oklahoma	56	57	+1	0.97
Oregon	83	83	0	---
South Dakota	67	100	+33	0.35
Utah	89	33	-56	0.05.
Washington	88	83	-5	0.76
Wyoming	33	100	+67	0.25

Note: No limits represents races at which point state limits had not been enacted or had been repealed.
(Data compiled by author from Jacobson Challenger Quality Measures)

The analyses, presented in Tables 6.4 and 6.5, respectively, appear to confirm that limits have a positive effect on quality levels. Table 6.4 shows that in nine (out of 21) cases, the introduction of limits increased the proportion of open seat races with at least one experienced candidate. We observe a decrease in the proportion of high-quality candidates after limits are introduced in nine cases: Arkansas, California, Florida, Louisiana, Missouri, Nevada, Ohio, Utah, and Washington. In the other three cases for which data is available, there was no change post-limits. Each of these states, however, had pre- and post-limits maximum of 100%. The data reported in Table 6.4 indicate, however, that the differences of means before and after limits were in effect achieved significance in three states (Louisiana decreased $p < 0.10$; Ohio decreased $p < 0.05$; Utah decreased $p < 0.10$), so the conclusions we can draw from the analysis are limited.

The figures in Table 6.5 indicate that the proportion of open seat races with at least one former state legislator decreased after limits were introduced in nine states (Arizona, Colorado, Florida, Louisiana, Nevada, Ohio, Oregon, South Dakota, and Utah). In every other case for which data is available, the mean proportion after limits increased (except Montana and Arkansas, where there was no change). While the data are severely more limited (due to the small number of open seat races in states), the analyses provide some additional, preliminary

TABLE 6.5 Proportion of Open Seat Races with At Least One Candidate Who Was Previously State Legislator, Given Limits in Places vs. No Limits By State (1972–2018)

	No Limits	Limits in Place	Change	Probability (p-value)
Arizona	50	47	-3	0.87
Arkansas	33	33	0	---
California	48	65	+17	0.08.
Colorado	85	73	-12	0.47
Florida	67	53	-14	0.23
Idaho	86	100	+14	0.57
Louisiana	40	0	-40	0.09.
Maine	71	100	+29	0.3
Massachusetts	53	100	+47	0.35
Michigan	61	62	+1	0.94
Missouri	57	62	+5	0.81
Montana	100	100	0	---
Nebraska	67	100	+33	0.49
Nevada	88	0	-88	0**
Ohio	71	62	-8	0.58
Oklahoma	31	43	+12	0.59
Oregon	67	50	-17	0.56
South Dakota	50	0	-50	0.21
Utah	67	33	-33	0.31
Washington	65	83	+19	0.39
Wyoming	33	100	+67	0.25

Note: No limits represents races at which point state limits had not been enacted or had been repealed.
(Data compiled by author from Jacobson Challenger Quality Measures)

evidence that the introduction of limits has a positive effect on the overall levels of candidate quality in open seat races.

Conclusions

The evidence presented in this analysis suggests that the introduction of state legislative term limits is likely increasing electoral competition in races for the U.S. House of Representatives, especially in races against incumbents. The data also offer support for the contention that state legislative term limits increase electoral competition in open seat races by producing higher proportions of former state legislators as candidates in these races. However, few of these findings rest on solid empirical footing. Most of the results do not achieve significance at conventional levels. In the chapters that follow, the impact of state legislative term limits on levels of challenger quality will be investigated more systematically.

If the findings of this preliminary exploration hold up, the implication is that state legislative term limits are making—or at least are likely to make—U.S. House elections more competitive by producing high-quality challengers to run against

TABLE 6.6 State Legislative Term Limits and Re-election Rates (U.S. House)

	# States with Term Limits	% Incumbents from States with Limits	House Reelection Rates
1972	0	0	98
1974	0	0	90
1976	0	0	97
1978	0	0	95
1980	0	0	92
1982	0	0	94
1984	0	0	96
1986	0	0	98
1988	0	0	99
1990	0	0	96
1992	3	2.9	94
1994	6	6.8	91
1996	8	20.7	94
1998	11	24.4	98
2000	15	33.8	98
2002	15	35.3	99
2004	13	35.1	99
2006	14	35.6	95
2008	14	36.3	95
2010	15	36.5	86
2012	15	34.7	95
2014	15	36.3	97
2016	15	36.3	98
2018	15	38.8	92

(Data compiled by author from Jacobson Challenger Quality Measures)

incumbents. To be sure, incumbents remain solidly secure for the time being. Table 6.6 shows that incumbent reelection rates, for example, have not experienced any noteworthy decline since limits began to take effect in 1996. Nevertheless, if the quality of U.S. House challengers increases overall—partly as a result of limits—these races may become more competitive and incumbents may have greater reason to be "running scared." Such expectations are dampened by the results of the analyses presented in Chapter 8, however, which reveal that state legislative term limits exert no discernible effect on challenger quality.

7
STATES OF AMBITION

Aggregate Challenger Quality in the U.S. by State, 1972–2018

Do some states consistently recruit greater proportions of high-quality challengers in elections for the U.S. House of Representatives while other states do so less frequently? If so, what explains this variation? This chapter aims to answer this question by examining state-level variation in mean aggregate levels of high-quality challengers.

During the period from 1972–2018, across all states, the average proportion of high-quality challengers was 26.6% (standard deviation.= 12.2; Min = 9.8; Max = 60.5).[1] Yet certain states consistently recruit, on average, fewer experienced challengers relative to other states. In Maine, for example, 60.5% of all challengers during this period previously held elective office and were thus high-quality. About half of the challengers in New Mexico and Alaska, on average, are high-quality. By contrast, only 13–14 out of 100 challengers on average in both Georgia and Florida have previous successful electoral experience, only 9–12 percent in Tennessee California, or Illinois.

An analysis of the dynamics of challenger quality across states reveals some interesting patterns. Despite considerable variation in overall levels of challenger quality within and across states between 1972 and 2018, the analysis indicates that there has been no statistically significant change ($p < 0.05$) in the overall challenger quality in most (39) states. In fact, challenger quality in congressional elections has increased in just one state: Arkansas. By contrast, statistically significant declines in challenger quality can be observed in ten states: Delaware, Indiana, Maryland, Massachusetts, New Jersey, North Carolina, South Carolina, Tennessee, Vermont, and Virginia.

Even as candidates assess national and district-level strategic considerations when making decisions about whether or not to seek to unseat incumbents, there

DOI: 10.4324/9781315164649-7

78 States of Ambition

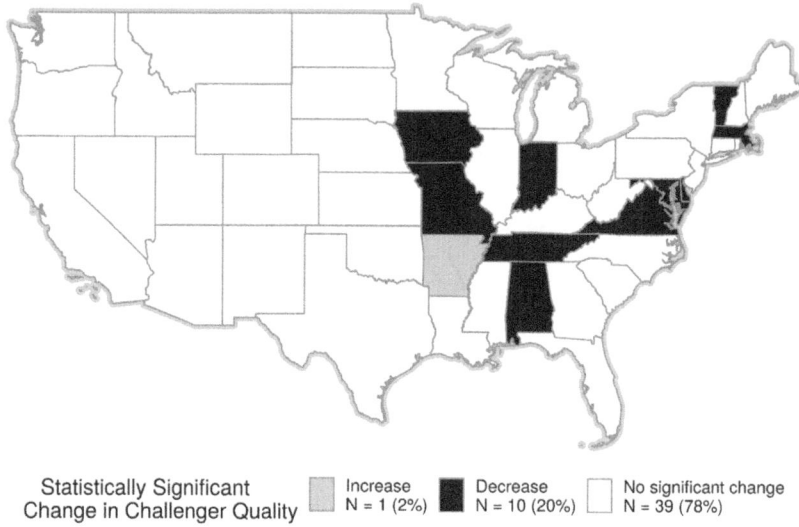

FIGURE 7.1 Challenger Quality Dynamics by State (1972–2018) (Map)

TABLE 7.1 Challenger Quality Dynamics by State (1972–2018)

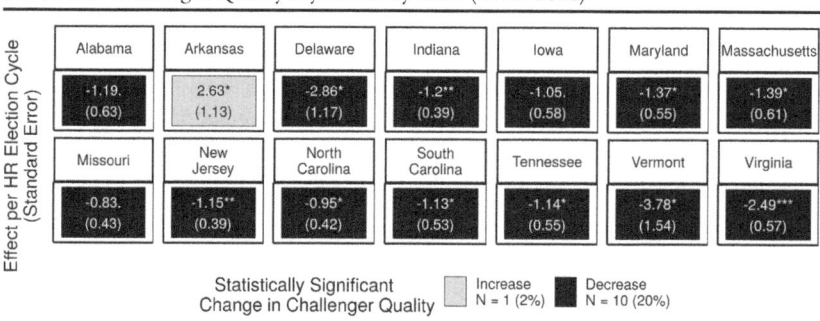

*** p<.001 ** p<.01 * p<.05, . p < 0.10
Note: No statistically significant change in other states.

appears to be considerable state-level variation in the degree to which states can recruit high-quality challengers. A closer analysis of the data may reveal clearer challenger recruitment patterns in states across the country.

The variation we observe in overall proportions of high-quality challengers across states during this period may be explained by a variety of state-level structural or institutional factors. Chapter 3 describes three factors that may be relevant to this question: State legislative professionalization, the level of party competition

TABLE 7.2 High-Quality Challengers by Level of State Legislative Professionalism*

	Citizen	Hybrid	Professional
% Experienced Challengers (2012)	23.8	21.4	22.8

*Difference between categories is not significant at conventional levels.

TABLE 7.3 High-Quality Challengers by Level of Party Competition*

	One-Party	Two-Party
% Experienced Challengers (2012)	14	22.6

*Difference between categories is significant at p<.10.

TABLE 7.4 High-Quality Challengers by State Legislative Term Limits*

	No Limits	Limits in Place
% Experienced Challengers (2012)	17.1	15.6

*Difference between categories is not significant at conventional levels.

in each state, and state legislative term limits. I expect that each of these factors will impact the overall proportion of high-quality challengers recruited in states to challenge incumbents. I will conduct preliminary analyses to test each of these expectations with data from the 2012 elections in the analyses that follow. I describe my expectations below.

Tables 7.2 –7.4 offer preliminary evidence about the impact of each of these factors. In Chapter 8, these factors will be incorporated into an individual-level model to predict the emergence of a high-quality challenger. The analyses below, however, provide some initial insights about each factor's impact.

State Legislative Professionalization. Scholars categorize state legislatures by their degree of professionalization, a measure based on such features as session length, size of legislative operations (staff sizes, etc.), and salary. Substantial differences emerge between state legislatures with respect to these dimensions. State legislatures in California and New York, for example, meet virtually full-time and legislators receive compensation of $114,700 and $79,400 per year, respectively, while in North Dakota and Montana legislators meet for only a few months every other year and earn $9,400 and $7,000 per year respectively (Gray and Hanson 2004: 157). Legislatures in nine states are categorized as fully "professionalized," based on these criteria. State assemblies in 25 states are partly professionalized and often categorized as "hybrid" legislatures. The remaining d6 state legislatures are considered "citizen legislatures" (Gray and Hanson 2004).

Scholars suggest (Canon 1990; see Chapter 3) that potential challengers for the U.S. House, especially experienced politicians who may be serving as state legislators, may be satisfied with opportunities within their states, particularly in states where legislatures are professional. Thus, we can expect an inverse relationship between state legislative professionalization and high-quality challenger recruitment. That is, we can hypothesize that states with professional legislatures should recruit fewer high-quality challengers, on average, than states with hybrid legislatures and that the overall proportions of high-quality challengers in states with hybrid legislatures should exceed those of citizen legislatures. The hypothesis is that greater state legislative professionalization should yield lower overall levels of experienced challengers in House elections.

The data presented in Table 7.2 appear to provide preliminary support for this hypothesis. This table focuses on 2012, the most recent year for which measures of state legislative professionalization were available. The bivariate analysis reveals that the overall proportion of high-quality challengers in U.S. House elections in states with citizen legislatures was 23.8% in 2012. As expected, the mean proportion of high-quality challengers in states with hybrid legislatures drops to 21.4%. Finally, 22.8% of challengers are experienced in states with professional legislatures. The differences between the categories are not significant at the conventional levels. These findings do hold up when we conduct individual-level analyses in Chapter 8, where the level of state legislative professionalism also appears to be unrelated to challenger quality.

Party Competition. Scholars generally recognize that party competition can influence state policies, voter turnout, and other key political elements (Key 1949; Gray and Hanson 2004). A commonly used and long-standing indicator of competition for control of state government is a measure developed by Austin Ranney (1976: 59–60; Gray and Russell 2004: 89). Ranney observes differences in the level of party competition across states, and this variation may also affect challenger quality. Canon (1990) suggests in his analysis (see Chapter 3) that healthier levels of party competition may positively affect challenger quality levels. Ranney creates a party competition index for each state. Using these indices, states can be grouped into two categories: States in which one party is dominant (either Democrat or Republican) and states with strong two-party competition between the major parties. Using this conceptualization as the variable for the degree of party competition in states, I hypothesize that the overall levels of challenger quality in states with two-party competition will be higher than in states where one party dominates the political scene.

The data presented in Table 7.3 appears to dispute this hypothesis. The results of the bivariate analysis indicate that the proportion of high-quality challengers in states with strong party competition is somewhat higher than the proportion we observe in states with weak party competition. On average, 14% of challengers in one-party states were experienced in 2012, compared to 22.6% of challengers in two-party states, a difference that is only marginally statistically significant ($p < 0.10$).

State Legislative Term Limits. Chapter 6 presented a more elaborate discussion of expectations, theory, and evidence of the impact of state legislative term limits on challenger quality levels. The results of the bivariate analysis displayed in Table 7.4 below, however, do not affirm that expectation that state legislative term limits exert a positive effect on challenger quality. Challenger quality in term-limited states in 2012 was slightly lower than in states with no state legislative term limits legislation in effect, although this difference is not statistically significant. In states with state legislative term limits legislation in effect 15.6% percent of challengers, in 2014, had prior elective experience, while about 17.1% of challengers in states with no state legislative term limits in effect were high-quality. This relationship is not significant at conventional levels, however, and does not hold up in individual-level analyses conducted in Chapter 8.

More detailed analyses of the independent effects of each of these variables will be tested in the individual-level model estimated in Chapter 8. Table 7.5, however, presents the results of two models that estimate the impact of each of

TABLE 7.5 State-level Institutional Determinants of Proportion of Experienced Challengers (2012)

Beta Coefficients (Standard Errors)	OLS Model Dependent Variable: *Mean Proportion of Experienced Challengers by State*	Logit Model Dependent Variable: *Experienced Challengers (0/1) by District*
Independent Variables		
State Leg. Professionalization	0.46 (4.86)	−0.01 (0.21)
Two-Party Competition	3.98 (7.28)	**0.52** (0.29)★
State Legislative Term Limits	0.50 (7.80)	0.30 (0.31)
Mean VIF	1.02	1.12
Adj. R^2 (OLS) Nagelkerke's Psuedo-R^2 (Logit)	−0.06	0.02
Num. obs.	49	319
F statistic	0.10	

★★★$p < 0.001$; ★★$p < 0.01$; ★$p < 0.05$; .$p < 0.1$.

the institutional factors discussed above on challenger experience levels in 2012. The left column presents a state-level, multivariate OLS model that tests these factors' effects on a state's proportion of high-quality challengers in 2012. The right column presents a district-level multivariate logit model that tests these factors' effects on whether the challenger in that district had any prior experience. The findings confirm most of the results of the bivariate analyses above. The effect of state legislative term limits is not statistically significant at conventional levels. In fact, the OLS coefficients reported in Table 7.5 do not reflect statistically significant influences of state legislative term limits, state legislative professionalization, or two-party competition on challenger quality. Among logit coefficients, only two-party competition presented a slight positive, marginally statistically significant association with challenger experience levels ($p < 0.10$). The results of these multivariate analyses weaken some of the initial evidence presented in earlier chapters that suggest a modest, positive impact of state legislative term limits on challenger quality. In the end, these preliminary findings remain about the same when we conduct the individual-level analyses in Chapter 8.

Conclusion

This chapter demonstrates substantial variation across states with respect to the overall level of challenger quality in U.S. House elections between 1972 and 2018. The results show that some states *do* consistently recruit lower levels of high-quality challengers while others consistently recruit higher proportions of experienced challengers. The results of both the bivariate and multivariate analyses suggest that state-level institutional features likely do not explain the variance we observe. As a preview, I note that these initial findings are largely confirmed in the district-level analyses conducted in the following chapter which consider the impact of each of these variables on the probability that a high-quality contender will emerge to challenge an incumbent.

Note

1 A detailed list of state by state statistics is available in appendix Table A7.1

8
EXPLAINING THE DECLINE IN CHALLENGER QUALITY, 1972–2018

Exploratory findings of the determinants of challenger quality may be telling, but we can draw conclusions about the impact of these factors on challenger quality with greater confidence by estimating individual-level models. Canon (1990) makes a strong argument for such an approach: "While their [Jacobson and Kernell] theory is intuitively plausible and supported by national-level data, the district-level link must be established to discover the factors that influence experienced candidates' decisions to run for higher office" (93). Many subsequent studies (summarized in Chapter 2) also adopted this approach.

This chapter develops and tests individual (district)-level models to predict the probability that a high-quality challenger will emerge to run against an incumbent. The following provides a summary of the anticipated effects of each of the variables based on the hypotheses developed in previous analyses.

Summary of Expected Effects

Variable	Effect
Lagged Incumbent Spending	−/+
Majority Status	+
Competitiveness	−
State Legislative Term Limits	+
Redistricting	−/+

I will also examine the influence of several other factors discussed in previous chapters, including the effect of such state-level institutional factors as the degree of party competition and the level of state legislative professionalism. The

DOI: 10.4324/9781315164649-8

TABLE 8.1 Summary Statistics

	Obs	Mean	Std. Dev.	Min	Max
Experienced Challenger	7882	0.2	0.4	0	1
Incumbent Spending (In logged 2018 dollars, prior election)	7514	13.46	1.02	8.52	16.96
Challenger Spending (In logged 2018 dollars; prior election)	5926	11.42	1.91	8.52	16.25
Incumbent Party in HR Majority	7882	0.57	0.5	0	1
Incumbent Party Strength in District (Prior Presidential Campaign)	7855	57.01	12.08	8.58	96.99
State legislative term limits	7882	0.18	0.38	0	1
Experienced Challenger (prior election)	6179	0.22	0.41	0	1
State Legislative Professionalism	6913	2.39	0.7	1	3
Party Competition	6864	0.57	0.33	0	1

following is a summary of the hypotheses and descriptions of the variables to be included in the models and their measurement. Table 8.1 reveals the summary statistics for the model variables.

Dependent Variable: Challenger Quality. My measure of quality is the dichotomous construction originally developed by Jacobson: Prior elective experience. The variable is coded 1 if the challenger had held prior elective office, 0 otherwise.

Independent Variables: *Campaign Costs – Lagged Incumbent Spending (logged)*.[1] The best indicator a potential challenger can use to estimate the anticipated cost of waging a competitive campaign against an incumbent (at time t) is to determine how much the incumbent spent in his previous campaign in the district (time $t-1$). Barring complications that can arise from redistricting (to be discussed below), lagged incumbent spending can serve as a functional approximation of the cost of a competitive campaign targeting voters in the same district. This amount, then (in logged dollars, in 2018 dollars), is used to measure the cost of a competitive campaign. Some incumbents (N = 4) and challengers (N = 839) were recorded as having spent zero dollars on their campaigns. This is improbable and more likely refers to having spent just a very small amount, such that no disclosures were required or reported. Further, zero cannot be log-transformed. To address this, I adopt the same approach used by Jacobson (2009), assuming when log-transforming that all candidates have spent at least $5,000, the Federal Election Commission's minimum reporting threshold, before adjusting for inflation. By replacing such values with $5,000, and then adjusting for inflation, this maintains the shape of the original distributions, permits log-transformation, and allows the analyses to retain valuable observations whose omission might otherwise skew results. Lagged Incumbent spending ranges from $0 to $23,105,000 with a mean of $1,038,900 and a standard deviation of $1,012,278. The logged calculation ranges from 8.52 to 16.96 logged dollars with a mean of 13.46 and a standard deviation of 1.02. I expect this variable to exert a negative effect on the dependent variable. Daunted by fundraising handicaps associated with challengers (see Chapter 4) and by the necessity to finance a competitive and viable campaign, I hypothesize that greater incumbent expenditures in the previous campaign will deter experienced candidates from entering the race, thereby depressing the probability that a high-quality challenger decides to run.

Greater incumbent spending may also suggest vulnerability, however. Incumbents who assess their prospects for victory as tenuous should spend more to remain in office. If this is the case, potential challengers should be encouraged by greater incumbent spending in the previous election cycle. These expectations generate the hypothesis that the impact of lagged incumbent spending may depend on how spending is perceived by potential candidates. If potential challengers perceive the level of incumbent spending in the previous cycle as a sign of viability, then higher incumbent spending will signal vulnerability and increase the probability of an experienced challenger in the next election. If high incumbent spending is viewed simply as an indicator of campaign cost, then higher spending will signal a more expensive campaign and depress the likelihood of an experienced challenger in the subsequent cycle.

Challenger Spending. Challengers' strategic entry calculations may also be affected by challenger expenditures in the previous election cycle. Greater spending by the challenger in the previous cycle may also be an indicator of the costliness of a campaign. As such, greater challenger spending in the previous cycle may signal a race that is more costly, thus depressing challenger quality levels. My measure of this variable is the challenger's expenditures in the previous election cycle (in logged 2018 dollars). The standard calculation of this variable ranges from $0 to $11,410,330 with a mean of $382,080 and a standard deviation of $715,045. The logged calculation ranges from 8.526 to 16.25 logged dollars with a mean of 11.42 and a standard deviation of 1.91. I imputed cases of challenger spending below $5,000 in the same way described for incumbent spending to accommodate logged spending.

Of course, greater challenger spending in the previous cycle may also signal stronger prospects for victory for the challenger. Greater challenger spending in the previous cycle may also indicate that the challenger had greater access to funds, most likely to occur when prospects for victory against the incumbent are stronger. Thus, it is also conceivable that greater challenger spending in the previous cycle will impact the overall challenger quality level in a positive way. These expectations help to generate the following hypothesis that the impact of lagged challenger spending may depend on how spending is perceived by potential candidates. If potential challengers believe challenger spending is an indicator of viability, then higher levels of challenger expenditure in the previous cycle will boost the probability of an experienced challenger in the subsequent cycle. If high spending is viewed simply as an indicator of campaign cost, then higher challenger spending in the previous cycle will signal a more expensive campaign and depress the probability of an experienced challenger in the next election.

Lagged spending variables are key components in my analytical setup. Nevertheless, I recognize that the model specification I introduce below makes it difficult to adequately test clear hypotheses that relate to the impact of lagged campaign spending on challenger quality in the subsequent election. The interactive model I introduce, as I will describe below, will make testing hypotheses about the effect of lagged spending clearer. Despite these limitations, I describe the hypotheses here to describe the intuition behind each.

Incumbent Party Strength in District (Competitiveness). Potential challengers will also seek to estimate their likelihood of winning. A useful indicator of the incumbent's likely performance in the election (at time *t*) is the incumbent party's electoral strength in the district. I measure district partisanship as the party's electoral performance in the most recent presidential election. This is the measure I use to estimate competitiveness. This variable ranges from 8.58% to 96.99%, with a mean of 57.01% and a standard deviation of 12.08%. I expect that higher voteshares for the incumbent's party in the previous presidential election will discourage subsequent opposition from experienced contenders, thereby exerting a negative impact on the probability of a high-quality challenger. I predict that greater incumbent party strength in the district, as determined by the share of the two-party vote of the incumbent's party presidential candidate in the most recent election, will discourage quality opposition and depress the probability of an experienced challenger in the subsequent cycle.

Majority Status. I expect that incumbents can argue that they can deliver greater benefits to the district when their party possesses majority status in the House of Representatives. I construct a dummy variable to test this hypothesis (coded 1 if the incumbent's party is in the majority, 0 otherwise). This variable's mean is 0.57, with a standard deviation of 0.50. I anticipate that when the incumbent's party is in the majority, the probability that experienced candidates emerge to challenge incumbents will be lower.

I hypothesize that when the incumbent's party enjoys majority status in the U.S. House of Representatives, the probability of a high-quality challenger will be lower than when the incumbent's party is in the minority, *ceteris paribus.*

Structural/Institutional Variables: State Legislative Term Limits. Chapter 6 presents a detailed discussion about the theoretical relationship anticipated to exist between state legislative term limits and challenger quality. The analysis also provides some preliminary results about this relationship. The theory and the findings presented above suggest that state legislative term limits exert a small, but positive, effect on challenger quality. Aggregate-level analyses presented appear to corroborate these results. Here I incorporate state legislative term limits as a variable in the individual-level analysis. The variable is measured dichotomously, coded 1 if the district is in a state with state legislative term limits legislation in effect during the election cycle, 0 otherwise. State legislative term limits has a mean of 0.18 and a standard deviation of 0.38. I hypothesize that this variable should increase the probability that a high-quality challenger opposes an incumbent.

I control for the quality of the challenger in the previous cycle in the analysis. I also control for the impact of time trends in these analyses by using year fixed effects in the models. To examine interparty differences, I conduct these analyses separately by party as well. In an individual-level model with lagged variables, redistricting becomes problematic. Strategic calculations based retrospectively on indicators of previous spending and competitiveness by potential challengers may be unrealistic if the district has been redrawn. Thus, in the individual-level analysis conducted here, districts that have been redrawn are excluded.

Empirical Strategy and Results

To examine the impact of each of these variables on the probability that a high-quality challenger emerges to contest an incumbent, I estimate a series of probit models. The model specification follows:

$$\Pr[\text{High-Quality Challenger}_{j,t}]$$
$$= f(\text{Constant})$$
$$+ \beta_1 * [\text{Lagged Incumbent Spending}_{j,t-1}]$$
$$+ \beta_2 * [\text{Lagged Challenger Spending}_{j,t-1}]$$
$$+ \beta_3 * [\text{Incumbent Party Strength (Competitiveness)}_{j,t-1}]$$
$$+ \beta_4 * [\text{Majority Status}_{j,t-1}]$$
$$+ \beta_5 * [\text{State Legislative term limits}_t]$$
$$+ \beta_6 * \text{Lagged Challenger Quality}_{j,t-1}$$
$$+ \beta_7 * [\text{Year1}]$$
$$+ \beta_8 * [\text{Year2}] + \ldots + \text{error}.$$

(where j = district and t = year of election cycle).

TABLE 8.2 Probability of an Experienced Challenger, 1974–2018 (Probit)

	Dependent Variable: High-Quality Challenger (0/1)	
	Coefficient[1]	Change in Probability[2]
Incumbent Spending	0.12**	0.01
(Prior election in logged 2018 dollars)	(0.04)	(0.007)
Challenger Spending	0.08***	0.023
(Prior election in logged 2018 dollars)	(0.02)	(0.004)
Incumbent Party in HR Majority	−0.20***	**−0.056**
	(0.05)	(0.014)
Incumbent Party Strength in District	−0.02***	−0.008
(Prior Presidential Election)	(0.00)	**(0.001)**
State Legislative Term Limits	−0.07	−0.018
	(0.06)	(0.017)
Experienced Challenger	0.36***	0.106
(Prior election)	(0.05)	**(0.018)**
Constant	−1.92***	
	(0.48)	
% Correctly Predicted	79.9	
Pseudo R-squared (Nagelkerke'S)	0.14	
Chi-squared (df)	471.1*** (24)	
Mean VIF	1.21	
Log Likelihood	−2214.53	
Deviance	4429.05	
Num. obs.	4904	

*** $p < 0.001$; ** $p < 0.01$; * $p < 0.05$, $p < 0.10$.
[1]Standard errors in parentheses. Spending data measured in logged 2018 dollars. Year fixed effects used but omitted from table. 1974 was the base fixed effects year. Redistricting years excluded (1982, 1992, 2002, 2012).
[2]Change in Prob. column indicates the median expected change in probability for a unit change in the explanatory variable, based on 1,000 simulations holding all other variables at their means. For the logged spending variables, it indicates that change in probability for a $1,000 increase.

Table 8.2 presents the overall results of the probit analysis when the sample includes both Democrats and Republicans. This model examines congressional districts between 1974 and 2018, excluding 1972 due to lagged variables as well as redistricting years (1972, 1982, 1992, 2002, 2012). The findings suggest higher incumbent spending in the previous election increases the probability that a high-quality challenger emerges to unseat the incumbent in the following cycle at a statistically significant level. The results indicate that challenger spending does exert a small but statistically significant (at $p < 0.001$ level) positive effect on the probability that a high-quality challenger emerges against the incumbent in the subsequent election. Majority status, as expected, exerts a statistically significant, negative effect on the dependent variable. The estimates presented in Table 8.2 reveal that when the incumbent's party holds majority status in the U.S. House of

Representatives, the probability that a high-quality challenger emerges to contest the incumbent in the general election is depressed by 5.7%. Similarly, the higher the incumbent's party strength is in the district (as indicated by district support for the incumbent party's presidential candidate in the most recent presidential election), the lower the likelihood that an experienced challenger contests the incumbent. The results show that for each one-percentage point increase in the incumbent party's district strength, the probability that a high-quality challenger appears falls by 0.8%.

The findings reveal little evidence, however, that state legislative term limits affect challenger quality. The state legislative term limits variable does not even come close to achieving conventional levels of significance. These results contradict evidence presented in earlier chapters about the effect of state legislative term limits on challenger quality. The presence of an experienced challenger in the previous cycle also raises the probability that an experienced contender emerged in the subsequent cycle. The negative coefficient for the time-trend terms confirms the overall pattern of decline that previous analyses have suggested.

Results by Party

Table 8.2 presents overall results of the district-levels analysis. To examine any differences between parties, I conducted parallel analyses separately by party. The results are presented in Table 8.3.

Data reported in Table 8.3 reveal some interparty differences, and some similarities, in the impact of the key explanatory variables in the analysis. The results of the estimation indicate that incumbent spending in the previous cycle is positively related to challenger quality in the subsequent race, but only for Democratic incumbents. Additionally, the estimates suggest the effect would differ across parties, depressing the probability of a high-quality challenger against Republican incumbents by 10.2% but increasing the probability in races against Democratic incumbents by 0.3%. This supports the idea that as a Democratic incumbent spends more in the previous election, challengers see this as an opportunity to dethrone the incumbent.

Challenger spending in the previous cycle does impact challenger quality in both Republican and Democratic races that involve incumbents, exerting a statistically significant, positive effect on the dependent variable. The data indicate that for each $1,000 increase in challenger spending in an average race in the previous election, the likelihood that an experienced challenger emerges against an incumbent increases by 1.7% for a Democratic candidate and 2.4% for a Republican candidate.

Majority status does appear to be related to the probability that experienced candidates emerge to unseat incumbents. Majority status decreases the likelihood that a high-quality challenger emerges against a Democratic incumbent (by 7.9%)

TABLE 8.3 Probability of an Experienced Challenger, by Party, 1974–2018 (Probit)

Dependent Variable High-Quality Challenger (0/1)

	Democratic Incumbent		Republican Incumbent	
	Coefficient[1]	Change in Probability[2]	Coefficient	Change in Probability
Incumbent Spending *(Prior election in logged 2018 dollars)*	**0.15**** (0.05)	0.003 (0.004)	**−0.11*** (0.05)	−0.102 (0.03)
Challenger Spending *(Prior election in logged 2018 dollars)*	**0.08***** (0.02)	0.017 (0.002)	**0.09**** (0.02)	0.024 (0.004)
Incumbent Party in HR Majority	−0.34 (0.18)	−0.079 (0.044)	**−0.36*** (0.17)	−0.104 (0.047)
Incumbent Party Strength in District *(Prior Presidential Election)*	−0.01 (0.00)	**−0.03***** (0.00)	−0.007 (0.001)	**−0.03***** (0.00)
State Legislative Term Limits	−0.01 (0.10)	−0.004 (0.021)	**−0.18*** (0.08)	−0.048 (0.022)
Experienced Challenger *(Prior Election)*	**0.30***** 0.07)	0.073 (0.019)	**0.42***** (0.07)	0.128 (0.024)
Constant	**−2.19**** (0.67)		**1.82*** (0.76)	
% Correctly Predicted	82.4		77.5	
Pseudo R-squared (Nagelkerke's)	0.20		0.12	
Chi-squared (df)	334.9***(22)		194.4***(22)	
Mean VIF	1.96		1.94	
Log Likelihood	−1059.84		−1117.16	
Deviance	2119.67		2234.31	
Num. obs.	2624		2280	

*** $p < 0.001$; ** $p < 0.01$; * $p < 0.05$.

[1] Standard errors in parentheses. Spending data measured in logged 2018 dollars. Year fixed effects used but omitted from table. 1974 was the base fixed effects year. Fixed effects years 2004 through 2008 omitted because of colinearity. Redistricting years excluded (1982, 1992, 2002, 2012).

[2] Change in Prob. Column indicates the median expected change in probability for a unit change in the explanatory variable, based on 1,000 simulations holding all other variables at their means. For the logged spending variables, it indicates that change in probability for a $1,000 increase.

and also decreases the probability that a high-quality challenger emerges to unseat a Republican incumbent (by 10.4%).

Incumbent party strength in the district decreases the likelihood that experienced challengers contest incumbents consistently across both parties. For each unit increase in lagged incumbent party strength in the district, the probability that an experienced Republican challenger contests a Democratic incumbent drops by 1%. Similarly, for each unit increase in lagged incumbent party strength in the district, the likelihood that a high-quality Democratic challenger emerges against a Republican incumbent decreases by 0.7%.

The coefficients reported in Table 8.3 show that state legislative term limits may be associated with the probability that an experienced challenger contests the incumbent, but mainly for Republicans. The signs of the coefficients, however, suggest that the impact would likely be negative for both parties, rather than the hypothesized positive impact. The control for the quality of the challenger in the previous election exerts a significant, positive effect in both parties.

State-Level Structural and Institutional Features

Analyses above, and in the preceding chapters, have investigated the impact of state legislative term limits on challenger quality. In Chapter 7, I identified and conducted preliminary investigations about the influence of two other structural or institutional factors that may affect the likelihood that experienced challengers emerge to contest congressional incumbents: State legislative professionalism and party competition in a state. In Chapter 7, I conducted some initial analyses to investigate the effects of these institutional features on challenger quality. The results of these basic tests suggest that the overall proportion of high-quality challengers was almost identical in two-party states in 2012. The influence of state legislative professionalization was equally weak.

To conduct a more rigorous test of the impact of these two state-level institutional features on challenger quality, I incorporate them as additional explanatory variables in the individual-level analysis, focusing in on the years 1974 to 2012, for which these key variables were available. Based on the theoretical suppositions described in Chapter 7, I develop and test the following hypotheses with respect to each feature.

State Legislative Professionalism. I use a standard measure of state legislative professionalism that is prevalent in the literature, categorizing states as either professional (coded 3, the most professional), hybrid (coded 2), or citizen legislatures (coded 1) (Gray and Hanson 2004). The mean of this variable is 2.39 with a standard deviation of 0.70. I posit that higher levels of state legislative professionalism will depress the probability of a high-quality challenger, *ceteris paribus*.

Party Competition. Based on the standard categorization of states as either states in which one party is dominant or states in which both major parties are competitive (as developed by Ranney; see Gray and Hanson 2004), I classify states as one-party (coded 0) or two-party (coded 1). The mean of this variable is 0.57 with a standard deviation of 0.33. I hypothesize that higher levels of two-party competition in a state will increase the probability of a high-quality challenger, *ceteris paribus*.

To investigate the independent impact of each of these variables, I estimate a probit model that includes the variables used in the previous analysis, adding these two variables. The results of the analyses are presented in Tables 8.4 and 8.5. Table 8.4 displays the results of the estimation when the observations include both

TABLE 8.4 Probability of an Experienced Challenger, 1974–2012 (Probit)

	Dependent Variable: *High-Quality Challenger (0/1)*	
	Coefficient[1]	Change in Probability[2]
Incumbent Spending	**0.11***	0.012
(Prior election in logged 2018 dollars)	(0.04)	(0.008)
Challenger Spending	**0.08****	0.023
(Prior election in logged 2018 dollars)	(0.02)	(0.004)
Incumbent Party in HR Majority	**−0.25****	−0.068
	(0.05)	(0.016)
Incumbent Party Strength in District	**−0.02****	−0.008
(Prior Presidential Campaign)	(0.00)	(0.001)
State legislative term limits	−0.03	−0.008
	(0.08)	(0.02)
Experienced Challenger	**0.34****	0.1
(Prior Election)	(0.06)	(0.019)
State Legislative Professionalism	**−0.11****	−0.036
	(0.03)	(0.012)
Two-Party State	**−0.13**	−0.037
	(0.08)	(0.02)
Constant	**−1.29***	(0.52)
%Correctly Predicted	79.4	
Pseudo R-squared (Nagelkerke's)	0.15	
Chi-squared (df)	404.6***(23)	
Mean VIF	1.18	
Log Likelihood	−1904.03	
Deviance	3808.07	
Num. obs.	4148	

*** p < 0.001; ** p < 0.01; *p < 0.05.
[1]Standard errors in parentheses. Spending data measured in logged 2018 dollars. Nebraska was omitted because of lack of a Ranney-Index. Year fixed effects used but omitted from table. 1974 was the base fixed effects year. Fixed effects years 2004 through 2008 omitted because of colinearity. Redistricting years excluded (1982, 1992, 2002, 2012).
[2]Change in Prob. Column indicates the median expected change in probability for a unit change in the explanatory variable, based on 1,000 simulations holding all other variables at their means. For the logged spending variables, it indicates that change in probability for a $1,000 increase.

Democrats and Republicans. The findings suggest there is a statistically significant influence that state legislative professionalism likely exerts on the probability that a high-quality challenger contests an incumbent. Consistent with the hypotheses advanced above, the effect is negative.

Table 8.5 displays the results by party when the model is estimated including the two additional variables. These results suggest that most variables have similar

TABLE 8.5 Probability of an Experienced Challenger, by Party, 1974–2018 (Probit)

Dependent Variable High-Quality Challenger (0/1)

	Democratic Incumbent		Republican Incumbent	
	Coefficient[1]	Change in Probability[2]	Coefficient	Change in Probability
Incumbent Spending	0.15**	0.004	−0.19**	−0.077
(Prior election in logged 2018 dollars)	(0.05)	(0.005)	(0.06)	(0.034)
Challenger Spending	0.08**	0.017	0.08**	0.025
(Prior election in logged 2018 dollars)	(0.02)	(0.002)	(0.02)	(0.003)
Incumbent Party in HR Majority	−0.28	−0.067	−0.38*	−0.106
	(0.18)	(0.049)	(0.17)	(0.044)
Incumbent Party Strength in	−0.03***	−0.01	−0.04***	−0.005
District	(0.00)	(0.001)	(0.01)	(0.002)
(Prior Presidential Election)				
State legislative term limits	0.00	0.00	−0.10	−0.029
	(0.11)	(0.025)	(0.10)	(0.029)
Experienced Challenger	0.29***	0.07	0.40***	0.126
(Prior Election)	(0.08)	(0.021)	(0.08)	(0.026)
State Legislative Professionalism	−0.03	−0.007	−0.20***	−0.007
	(0.05)	(0.012)	(0.05)	(0.012)
Two-Party State	−0.22*	−0.053	0.09	−0.054
	(0.11)	(0.025)	(0.11)	(0.026)
Constant	−2.03**		3.75***	
	(0.69)		(0.89)	
%Correctly Predicted	81.9		76.8	
Pseudo R-squared (Nagelkerke's)	0.19		0.14	
Chi-squared (df)	290.5***(21)		175.5***(21)	
Mean VIF	1.86		1.79	
Log Likelihood	−957.01		−908.40	
Deviance	191401		1816.81	
Num. obs.	2315		1833	

*** $p < 0.001$; ** $p < 0.01$; * $p < 0.05$.

[1] Standard errors in parentheses. Spending data measured in logged 2018 dollars. Nebraska was omitted because of lack of a Ranney-Index. Year fixed effects used but omitted from table. 1974 was the base fixed effects year. Fixed effects years 2004 through 2008 omitted because of collinearity. Redistricting years excluded (1982, 1992, 2002, 2012).

[2] Change in Prob. Column indicates the median expected change in probability for a unit change in the explanatory variable, based on 1,000 simulations holding all other variables at their means. For the logged spending variables, it indicates that change in probability for a $1,000 increase.

effects across parties. One difference is that lagged incumbent spending boosts the likelihood of an experienced challenger against a Democratic incumbent at a statistically significant level ($p < 0.001$) but decreases the likelihood of an experienced challenger facing a Republican incumbent ($p < 0.01$). Lagged challenger spending is significant and boosts the likelihood of experienced Republicans challengers ($p < 0.01$) and Democratic challengers ($p < 0.01$). Incumbent party strength in the district depresses significantly the probability across parties, although the effect is statistically significant just for Republicans ($p < 0.05$). State legislative term limits appears to exert a negative effect consistently across parties, but does not consistently achieve significance at conventional levels. Lagged challenger quality also seems to be positively and significantly related to quality in both parties. State legislative professionalism appears to depress the probability that a quality challenger emerges in both parties, as expected, but the variable is significant at conventional levels only in contests with Republican incumbents. The estimates suggest state-level party competition exerts mixed effects: Negative and statistically significant for Democrats, but positive and statistically insignificant at conventional levels for Republicans.

Explaining the Decline in Challenger Quality, 1972–2018

The puzzle that inspired this study was to explain the decline in overall levels of challenger quality observed in contested elections for the U.S. House of Representatives between 1972 and 2018. While still puzzling, this observation would have been less contentious if the decline in challenger quality had coincided with a corresponding increase in the level of experienced candidates contesting open seats for the House. A simplistic explanation would have been that politicians had become increasingly "strategic" over time (Jacobson and Kernell 1981), opting increasingly to throw their proverbial hats into the ring when the prospects for victory were strongest. But this is not the case. The decline in challenger quality did not occur at a time when quality in open seat races grew. Thus, the question remained: Why did challenger quality decline between 1972 and 2018?

I identified several factors that I believe to be related to the level of challenger quality in congressional elections. Several of these variables have been previously investigated by scholars whose research has yielded many useful insights about challenger quality. Others, such as the effects of campaign spending and state legislative term limits have not been included in previous work. In the end, my aim was to resolve the puzzle of dwindling quality. I hypothesized (in Chapter 3) that the decline in challenger quality could be explained by rising campaign costs. I suspected that increasingly expensive campaigns discouraged high-quality candidates from running against incumbents. Evidence presented in Chapter 4 demonstrates that campaign costs, as reflected in campaign spending, rose substantially for both challengers and incumbents during the period of this study. Yet the analyses that followed yielded inconclusive results about the relationship between campaign spending and challenger quality. The individual-level analyses reveal there may be partisan differences in the effects exerted by incumbent spending; incumbent spending exerts a significant effect only in the Democratic incumbent model.

Challenger spending exerts a statistically significant effect on quality consistently in each of the individual-level models, but the effect is positive. The predicted probabilities of a high-quality challenger at differing values of lagged challenger spending, holding all other variables at their means, displayed in Figure 8.1 affirm this result. As such, I find no support for my hypothesis that the decline in challenger quality can be accounted for by rising campaign costs.

I do, however, find clear and consistent support for the alternative hypothesis that the decline in quality during this period results from a corresponding decline in competitiveness in contested congressional elections against incumbents during this period. The results of the district-level analyses provide evidence that competitiveness is related positively to challenger quality. As competitiveness increases (indicated by a decrease in district support for the incumbent's party) challenger quality should rise. As competitiveness declines, however, the probability of a high-quality challenger drops. Data presented in Figure 8.2 confirm this claim. Figure 8.2 displays the predicted probabilities of a high-quality

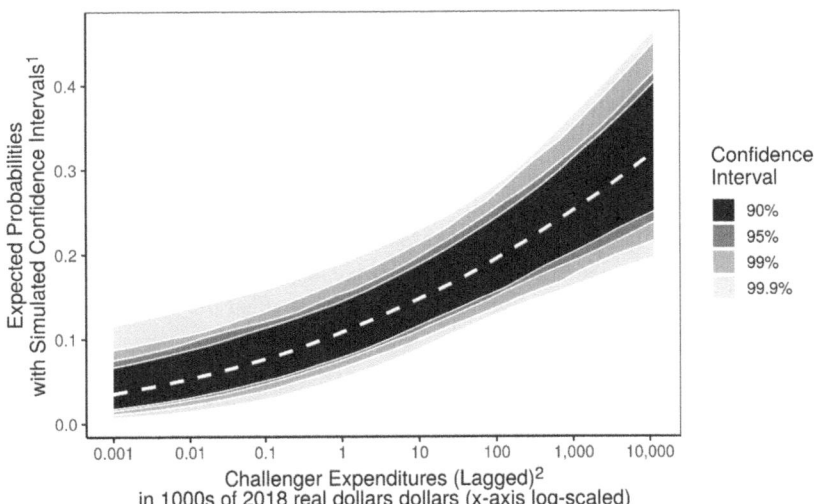

[1] Dashed line depicts median expected probability, while bands depict confidence intervals based on 1000 simulations in the Zelig package in R.

[2] Challenger expenditures were varied from 0 to the max observed value of $11,410,332, while holding all other independent variables at their mean. Based on model in Table 8.2.

FIGURE 8.1 Probabilities of Experienced Challenger by Challenger Spending

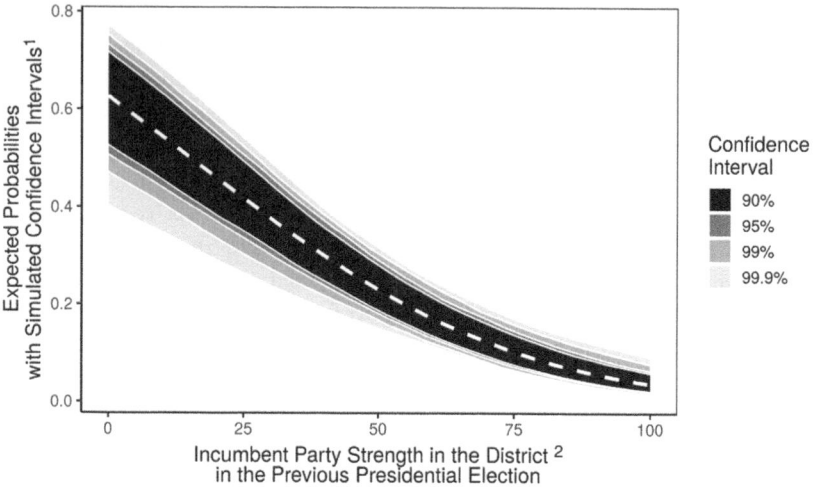

FIGURE 8.2 Probabilities of Experienced Challenger by Incumbent Party Strength

challenger for various values of incumbent party strength in the district, holding other variables at their mean. The evidence presented visually in Figure 8.2 confirms that higher levels of partisan support for the incumbent's party in the district depress the likelihood that an experienced challenger emerges to take on the incumbent.

An alternative method to show the effect of a unit change in the independent variable in a probit analysis is to evaluate $Pr(Y=1)$ for several different, arbitrarily selected values (a1, a2, a3, where a1 < a2 < a3) of the key explanatory variables (Nagler 1995). Such an analysis shows the effect on the probability of Y being equal to 1 as the independent variable increases from a1 to a2 to a3. By allowing the values of another key independent variable to vary, we can also determine how various combinations of two different variables affect the probability of the dependent variable taking on the value 1.

The results of such an analysis are presented in Table 8.6. The cell entries report predicted probabilities of a high-quality challenger for different combinations of the two key independent variables (lagged incumbent party strength in the district and lagged challenger spending), holding the values of all other relevant variables constant at their means. (Predicted probabilities were determined using statistical simulation in the Zelig package in R. See below.) The rows in the table represent three different levels of incumbent party strength in the district (percent) (lagged): 52, 56, and 60. The columns represent three different levels of challenger spending in the previous cycle (in thousands of

Explaining the Decline in Quality   97

TABLE 8.6 Expected Probability of Experienced Challenger for selected values of Lagged Challenger Spending and Incumbent Party Strength in the Districts

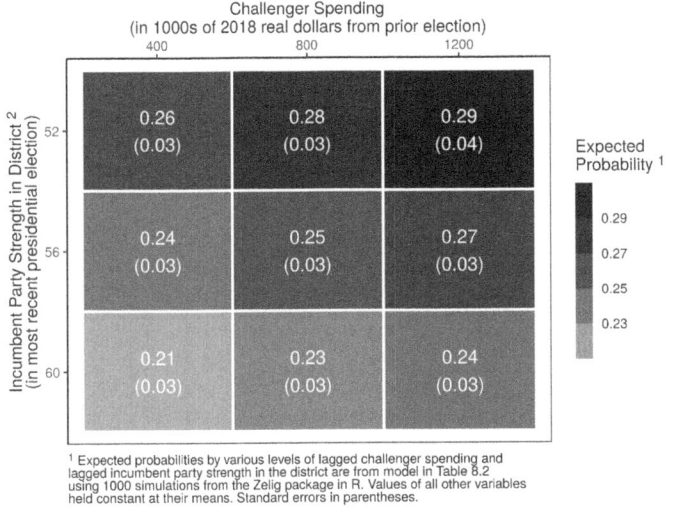

[1] Expected probabilities by various levels of lagged challenger spending and lagged incumbent party strength in the district are from model in Table 8.2 using 1000 simulations from the Zelig package in R. Values of all other variables held constant at their means. Standard errors in parentheses.

[2] Challenger spending and incumbent party strength varied across values.

dollars): 400, 800, and 1,200. The predicted probabilities demonstrate that the likelihood of a quality challenger emerging to contest an incumbent declines as incumbent party strength in the district rises for all levels of previous challenger spending. The value noted in the upper left cell indicates that if the incumbent party's strength in the district in the district equals 52% and the previous challenger spent $400,000 (5.6 logged dollars), the probability of a high-quality challenger in the subsequent election in the district is 0.26. The cell just below reveals that if the incumbent party's strength in the district was four percentage points higher (56%) but challenger spending was kept at $400,000, the likelihood of a quality challenger emerging would drop to 0.24. Keeping challenger spending constant at $400,000 dollars but increasing incumbent party strength in the district an additional four percentage points (to 60%) would depress the likelihood of a quality challenger further in the next election (to 0.21). Moving to column two, where previous challenger spending is fixed at $800,000 (5.9 logged dollars), a similar pattern emerges. The predicated probability of a quality challenger drops from 0.28 when incumbent party strength in the district equals 52% to 0.23 when the incumbent party strength in the district rises to 60%. Similarly, when prior challenger spending is fixed at $1,200,000 (6.1 logged dollars), the predicated probability of a quality challenger drops from 0.29 when incumbent party strength in the district equals 52% to 0.24 when the incumbent party strength in the district rises to 60%.

98 Explaining the Decline in Quality

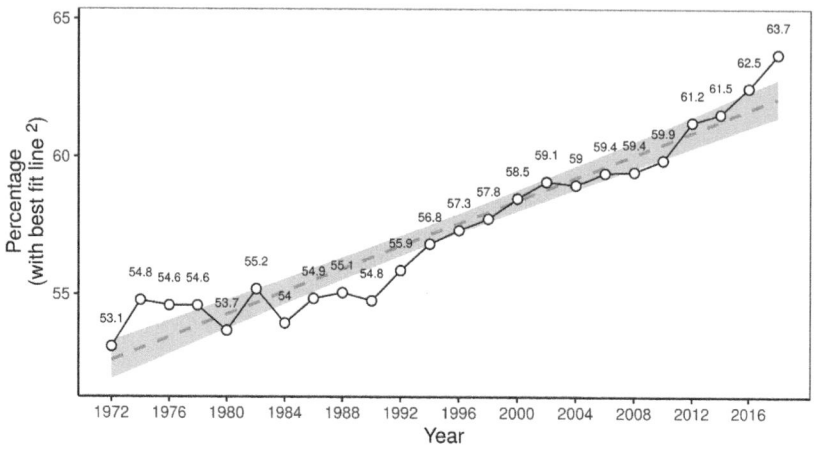

(Data compiled by author)

[1] Two-party share of the district's presidential vote for the incumbent's party candidate in the most recent presidential election.

[2] The dashed line gives the OLS regression line with 95% confidence intervals as determined by the data.

FIGURE 8.3 Incumbent Party Strength in District[1] (Mean), 1972–2018

Scholars have documented the steady decline in competitiveness in congressional elections (Abramowitz 2005; Ferejohn 1977). Data used for this study corroborate these findings. In my analysis, the incumbent's party strength in the district has increased significantly over time, effectively indicating that competitiveness has declined. Figure 8.3 depicts the dynamics of incumbent party's district strength during the period of my study. The data reported reveal that incumbent party strength in the district has increased systematically between 1972 and 2018, effectively indicating a decline in the level of competitiveness in congressional elections. A simple, OLS regression analysis (regressing mean district support for the incumbent's party on time and a constant) shows that district support for the incumbent party has increased by approximately 0.4 percentage points in each election cycle (Coefficient = 0.38; standard error = 0.04; $p < 0.0001$; N = 24).

Interpreting Statistical Results: Quantities of Interest

The results of these empirical analyses suggest the decline in competitiveness is the most reliable explanation for the decline in challenger quality I observe between 1972 and 2018. To provide more precise support for this claim, and to offer a more meaningful conclusion, I compute relevant quantities of interest to show how changes over time in the values of this key variable in my analysis (lagged incumbent party strength in the district) affected the observed change in challenger quality during the period of my study.

I use the Zelig package in R to conduct these analyses (King, Tomz, and Wittenberg 2003; Tomz, Wittenberg, and King 2000; Imai, King, and Lau 2008; Choirat et al. 2017). This software tool uses stochastic simulation techniques to draw simulations of the main and ancillary parameters from their asymptotic sampling distribution (Tomz et al. 2003: 5). Zelig then converts the simulated parameters into substantively interesting quantities, in this case, expected values, after the user sets values of the explanatory variables at desirable levels.

Setting all the relevant variables to their mean levels in 1974, the expected probability of a high-quality challenger in 1974 is 0.29 (standard error = 0.029). (Note: The analyses start in 1974 as a result of lagged values.) Changing the values of all the relevant variables to their mean levels in 2018, the expected probability of a high-quality challenger drops to 0.11 (standard error = 0.019). This finding suggests that the probability of a quality challenger in a given district dropped by 18 percentage points (standard error = 3.0) between 1974 and 2018.

How much of this decline is attributable to the change in incumbent party strength in the district? Recall that the expected probability of a quality challenger with all relevant variables set to their mean levels in 1974 is 0.29. To examine the effect of changes in lagged incumbent party strength in the district, I changed the values of this variable to its mean in 2018 (62.25) and predicted the probability of a high-quality challenger, holding the values of the other variables constant at their 1974 means. The predicted probability of an incumbent facing an experienced challenger at this level dropped to 0.11 (standard error = 0.02). The difference between these two quantities, 0.19 (standard error = 0.037) is the effect of incumbent party strength in the district going from its 1974 mean to its 2018 mean. These calculations suggest that the decline in competitiveness, as measured by changes in districts' partisan predispositions, accounts for virtually all of the total decline in the level of challenger quality observed between 1972 and 2018.

Examining the Effects of Spending in Context

The results of the analyses above suggest that higher challenger spending in an election exerts a positive effect on the probability of an experienced challenger in the subsequent cycle. The impact of lagged challenger spending cannot be properly estimated or interpreted, however, without understanding the context of the last election and the impact that challenger spending exerted. It may not be the case, *ceteris paribus*, that increased challenger spending in the last election causes the probability of an experienced challenger in the subsequent cycle to drop. However, increases in challenger spending in the previous cycle, holding the challenger's vote in the last election constant, may indeed decrease the likelihood of a quality challenger in the next cycle. Consider the following two scenarios: in the first case, the challenger got 45% of the two-party vote in the previous cycle and spent $500; in Case Two, the challenger also got 45% of the vote in the last cycle but spent $500,000. It is reasonable to expect that Case One would be more likely to lead to a high-quality challenger in the following cycle because it may demonstrate that the incumbent is more vulnerable than in Case Two.

This hypothetical situation suggests that the impact of lagged challenger spending on challenger quality in the next election may be conditional on the electoral results in the previous cycle. This section presents analyses that examine this claim. From this illustration I develop the hypothesis that the likelihood of a quality challenger will be low when challenger spending in the previous election was high and challenger performance in the same cycle was weak. Conversely, the likelihood of a quality challenger will be higher when challenger spending in the previous cycle was low and challenger performance in the same cycle was strong.

It may also be reasonable to expect that the marginal impact of lagged challenger quality on the probability of a quality challenger in the next cycle will decline as the incumbent's margin of victory increases. This line of reasoning suggests that lagged challenger spending may exert a stronger effect when the incumbent margin of victory in the previous election is low, in other words, when the election was more competitive, than when the election was a blowout (high incumbent victory margin). At some point, when the margin of victory is sufficiently high to make an incumbent defeat virtually impractical, any amount of challenger spending in the previous cycle may not be adequate to motivate a quality challenger. This line of reasoning generates the hypothesis that the effect of increases in challenger spending in the previous election on the probability of an experienced challenger in the next cycle will decline as the incumbent margin of victory increases.

Testing these hypotheses requires an interactive specification for the model. The most common technique used to test for interactive effects between two independent variables is to assume that such effects are multiplicative and to add a term equal to the product of the two variables as a separate independent variable in the model (Nagler 1991; Brambor, Clark, and Golder 2006; Braumoeller 2004). There are several advantages to including an interaction term that is relevant to the model. Among these is the fact that if an interaction does indeed exist and is excluded from the estimation, this introduces a specification error in the form of omitted variable bias. An estimation of a model that fails to account for the interaction will not provide an accurate estimate of the true relationship between the dependent and independent variables. A model that includes the interaction term provides a better description of the relationship between the independent and dependent variables (Friedrich 1982).

I will estimate such a model using an interaction term to investigate the effect of lagged challenger spending conditioned on challenger performance in that race. I use the *incumbent's margin of victory* in the previous cycle to measure challenger performance. The higher the incumbent's margin of victory in the previous cycle, the poorer the challenger performed. By itself, I expect that this term should exert a negative effect on the likelihood of an experienced challenger in the subsequent cycle as a higher margin of victory for the incumbent suggests greater electoral strength. Conversely, a lower margin of victory should increase the probability of a quality challenger in the next cycle because it suggests the incumbent may be vulnerable and the election competitive. This expectation yields the hypothesis that higher incumbent victory margins in the previous cycle will depress challenger quality in the subsequent election.

I create an interaction term between the incumbent margin of victory in the previous cycle and challenger spending in the same cycle.[2] I estimate two probit models to predict the probability of an experienced challenger. Model 1 presents the estimates when the dependent variable is a function of only the incumbent margin of victory, the spending terms, the relevant interactions, fixed year (election cycle) effects, and a constant. Model 2 presents the results of the model estimated in Table 8.2 with lagged incumbent margin of victory and the two interaction terms added to the model. The following equation presents details about the estimation of Model 2:

$\Pr[\text{High-Quality Challenger}_{j,t}]$

$= f(\text{Constant})$

$+ \beta_1 * [\text{Lagged Incumbent Spending}_{j,t-1}]$

$+ \beta_2 * [\text{Lagged Challenger Spending}_{j,t-1}]$

$+ \beta_3 * [\text{Incumbent Margin of Victory}_{j,t-1}]$

$+ \beta_4 * [\text{Incumbent Margin of Victory}_{j,t-1} \times \text{Lagged Incumbent Spending}_{j,t-1}]$

$+ \beta_5 * [\text{Incumbent Margin of Victory}_{j,t-1} \times \text{Lagged Challenger Spending}_{j,t-1}]$

$+ \beta_6 * [\text{Incumbent Party Strength (Competitiveness)}_{j,t-1}]$

$+ \beta_7 * [\text{Majority Status}_{j,t-1}]$

$+ \beta_8 * [\text{State legislative term limits}_t]$

$+ \beta_9 * [\text{Lagged Challenger Quality}_{j,t-1}]$

$+ \beta_{10} * [\text{Year1}] + \beta_{11} * [\text{Year2}] + \ldots + \text{error}.$

(where j = district and t = year of election cycle)

Interpreting the Estimates of the Interactive Model

The interactive model describes the relationship as a conditional relationship, meaning the effects of each of the key independent variables on the dependent variable vary according to the level of the other independent variable. In the presence of an interaction the coefficients on the main explanatory variables do not represent a constant effect of the independent variable on the dependent variable. β_1, β_2, and β_3 are not interpretable alone because they only represent a portion of the effect of the corresponding variable on the dependent variable. In other words, the value of b1 represents only part of the effect of lagged incumbent spending on the dependent variable. The remaining effect is in the interaction term. The interpretation of the relevant coefficients follows.

In the model presented above, β_1 represents the effect of lagged incumbent spending on the probability of a high-quality challenger when the incumbent margin of victory in the previous election is 0. β_2 tells us the effect of lagged challenger spending on the probability of an experienced challenger in the subsequent cycle when the incumbent margin of victory is 0. β_3 will represent the effect of lagged incumbent margin of victory on the probability of a quality challenger when spending is 0. In essence, since the scenarios are unlikely, these coefficients are essentially meaningless in this model. On the other hand, β_4 and β_5 capture the interactive effect of lagged spending and incumbent margin of victory on the probability of an experienced challenger. To determine the marginal impact of the key variable of interest on changes in the probability of a high-quality challenger in the subsequent election, one may take the derivative with respect to the variable of interest. To determine the marginal effect of lagged challenger spending, for example, the main, relevant spending variable, on changes in the probability of a high-quality challenger, one may take the derivative with respect to lagged challenger spending. The following expressions represent the marginal impact.

Marginal effect of Lagged Challenger Spending

$$\partial\left[P(Y=1)\right] / \partial\left[\text{Lagged Challenger Spending}\right] =$$

$$\beta_2 + \beta_5 * \text{Lagged Incumbent Margin of Victory}.$$

Marginal impact of Lagged Incumbent Spending

$$\partial\left[P(Y=1)\right] / \partial\left[\text{Lagged Incumbent Spending}\right] =$$

$$\beta_1 + \beta_4 * \text{Lagged Incumbent Margin of Victory}.$$

Marginal impact of Lagged Incumbent Margin of Victory

$$\partial\left[P(Y=1)\right] / \partial\left[\text{Lagged Incumbent Margin of Victory}\right] =$$

$$\beta_3 + \beta_4 * \text{Lagged Incumbent Spending}$$

$$+ \beta_5 * \text{Lagged Challenger Spending}.$$

Explaining the Decline in Quality   **103**

The results of the estimation are presented in Table 8.7. The findings confirm there exists an interactive effect between lagged challenger spending and lagged incumbent margin of victory. The estimated coefficient of the key interaction term (lagged challenger spending × lagged incumbent margin of victory) is significant in the negative direction. Challenger spending has a stronger reductive effect on the probability of a high-quality challenger as incumbent margin of victory in the last election increases.

The findings of Model 2 reveal several points as well. First, the addition of the margin of victory term and the two interaction terms does not appear to alter the effects of the other variables in the model. Moreover, the effects of the relevant terms (including the interaction terms) do not differ in direction from Model 1 when added to the fuller model.

Table 8.8 displays the proportion of high-quality challengers observed at combinations of two different levels (high and low) of lagged challenger spending and lagged incumbent margin of victory. "High" indicates values above the observed mean of the variable, while the "low" reflects values below the mean level. These data indicate that the presence of a high-quality challenger is generally higher when the challenger in the previous election performed strongly, relative to the incumbent, regardless of how much the challenger spent in the previous cycle. The results also show that the effect of challenger spending is stronger at the high (less competitive) level of incumbent victory margin than at the low (more competitive) level of incumbent performance in the last election.

The results of the analyses presented in Table 8.9 tell a similar story. These tables present the expected values of the probability of a high-quality challenger for selected levels of lagged incumbent spending, lagged challenger spending and lagged incumbent margin of victory with all other variables set to their mean levels. Values of expected probabilities were calculated using the Zelig package in R from Model 2 in Table 8.7. Table 8.9 displays the results in three panels when lagged incumbent spending is set at $400,000 (left panel), $800,000 (center panel), or $1,200,000 (right panel). The selected levels of lagged challenger spending are the same: $400,000, $800,000, and $1,200,000. The three levels of incumbent victory margin selected for the analyses are 5, 10, and 20.

The data presented in Table 8.9 confirm the limited effect of lagged incumbent spending: We observe few differences in the predicted probabilities across all combinations of lagged challenger spending and lagged incumbent margin of victory across the three panels. The results also confirm several other expectations developed above. First, the predicted probability of a quality challenger in an election is generally higher when challenger performance in the previous cycle was strong (in other words, when the incumbent victory margin was lower) for all levels of lagged challenger spending. Second, the effect of lagged challenger spending on the probability of a quality challenger in the subsequent election is negligible. This disputes the relationship hypothesized. Next, as expected (Hypothesis 8.8), the probability of a quality challenger is relatively low, 0.234, when the challenger

TABLE 8.7 Probability of an Experienced Challenger, 1974–2018

Dependent Variable High-Quality Challenger(0/1)

	Interaction Model		Interaction Model with controls	
	Coefficient[1]	*Change in Probability*[2]	*Coefficient*	*Change in Probability*
Incumbent Spending *(Prior election in thousands of 2018 dollars)*	0.00* (0.00)	0 (0)	0.00 (0.00)	0 (0)
Challenger Spending *(Prior election in thousands of 2018 dollars)*	0.00* (0.00)	0 (0)	0.00* (0.00)	0 (0)
Incumbent Margin of Victory *(Prior election)*	−0.02*** (0.00)	−0.009 (0.001)	−0.01*** (0.00)	−0.007 (0.001)
Incumbent Margin of Victory X Incumbent spending *(Prior election)*	−0.00 (0.00)	−0.008 (0.001)	−0.00* (0.00)	−0.006 (0.001)
Incumbent Margin of Victory X Incumbent spending *(Prior election)*	−0.00 (0.00)	−0.009 (0.001)	−0.00* (0.00)	−0.006 (0.001)
Incumbent Party in HR Majority			−0.11* (0.05)	−0.031 (0.013)
Incumbent Party Strength in District *(Prior Presidential Campaign)*			−0.01*** (0.00)	−0.005 (0.001)
State Legislative Term Limits			−0.08 (0.06)	−0.022 (0.017)
Experienced Challenger *(Prior Election)*			0.31*** (0.05)	0.087 (0.017)
Constant	0.02 (0.10)		0.54** (0.17)	

% Correctly Predicted	80.4	80.6
Pseudo R-squared (Nagelkerke's)	0.15	0.17
Chi-squared (df)	502.3***(23)	562.6***(27)
Mean VIF	1.76	1.51
Log Likelihood	−2194.15	−2160.84
Deviance	4388.31	4321.68
Num. obs.	4895	4887

*** $p < 0.001$; ** $p < 0.01$; * $p < 0.05$; $p < 0.10$.

[1] Standard errors in parentheses. Spending data measured in 1,000s of 2018 dollars. For interaction models, spending was not log-transformed. Redistricting years excluded (1982, 1992, 2002, 2012).

[2] Change in Prob. Column indicates the median expected change in probability for a unit change in the explanatory variable, based on 1,000 simulations holding all other variables at their means. For the logged spending variables, it indicates that change in probability for a $1,000 increase. For interactions, it indicates the change in probability given a $1,000 increase in spending and a 1% increase in the incumbent's margin of victory in the prior election.

106 Explaining the Decline in Quality

TABLE 8.8 Proportion of Experienced Challengers[1], by Levels of Incumbent Margin of Victory and Challenger Spending in Previous Election

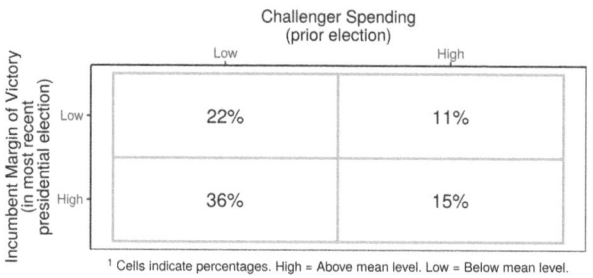

[1] Cells indicate percentages. High = Above mean level. Low = Below mean level.

TABLE 8.9 Expected Probability of Experienced Challengers for selected values of Lagged Challenger Spending and Lagged Incumbent Margin of Victory Given varying Lagged Incumbent Spending

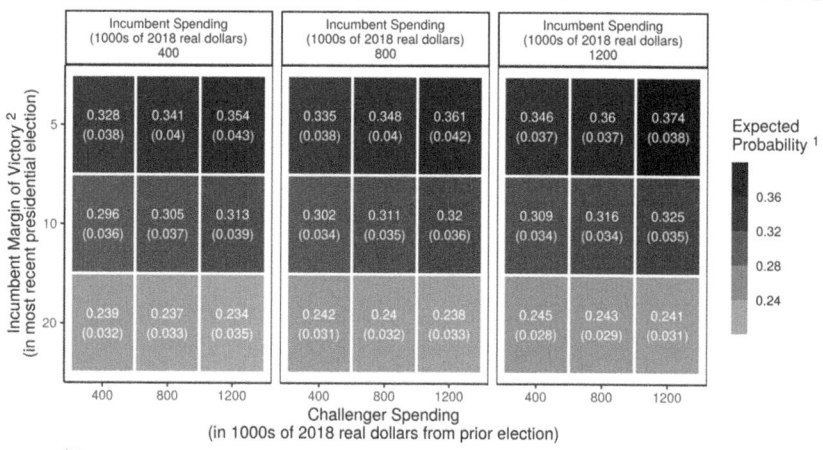

[1] Expected probabilities by various levels of lagged challenger spending, lagged incumbent margin of victory, and lagged incumbent spending are from model 2 in Table 8.7. Calculated using 1000 simulations from the Zelig package in R. Values of all other variables held constant at their means. Standard errors in parentheses.

[2] Challenger spending, incumbent margin of victory, and incumbent spending varied across three levels each.

performed weakly in the previous cycle despite high campaign expenditures ($1,200,000.) This is relatively low, comparatively to when the challenger performed strongly in the previous cycle while spending the same amount on the campaign, 0.354.

These analyses confirm the impact of challenger spending on the probability of a high-quality challenger in the subsequent election depends on *how* the challenger performs in the race relative to the incumbent. The complications of potential endogeneity that arise when prior electoral performance is introduced as a variable in the model suggest it may be imprudent to use this model to explain changes in challenger quality over time. Nevertheless, these analyses shed some light on the conditional nature of the effect of challenger spending in the last election on the likelihood that a quality challenger will emerge in the subsequent election cycle.

Discussion

The findings of the individual-level analyses presented in this chapter reveal several consistencies as well as inconsistencies across analyses. For one thing, the district-level models provide some evidence that incumbent spending is related to challenger quality, but the results are not statistically reliable and are inconsistent across parties. The probit models do confirm, however, that quality is responsive to challenger spending in the previous election: Higher challenger spending in the previous cycle increases the likelihood of an experienced challenger. This result implies that if the mean level of challenger spending increased between 1972 and 2018, as it did, then the number of high-quality challengers would have increased over the same period. But we observe no such increase in the emergence of high-quality challengers between 1978 and 2018. The growth in challenger spending between 1972 and 2018 cannot explain the pattern of declining challenger quality we observe over this period.

The district-level analysis also suggests that majority status is related to challenger quality; if the incumbent's party is in the majority in the chamber, the probability that an experienced challenger emerges is significantly lower (on average and in both parties). The district-level models also provide little support for a significant relationship between state legislative term limits and challenger quality.

The results of these analyses show that the stronger the challenger's party in the district, as measured by electoral performance in the last presidential election, the more likely we are to observe a high-quality challenger. This finding is consistent across parties. This obviously suggests that if the mean level of challenger party strength declined from 1972 to 2018, then the number of high-quality challengers emerging would also decline.

In this chapter, I demonstrate that an increase in incumbent party strength would have caused overall quality in U.S. House elections to drop over the period of this study. In tandem, the mean level of challenger party strength declined in this timeframe. Based on the analyses described in this chapter, the growth in incumbent party strength between 1972 and 2018 appears to be the main driver of the pattern of declining challenger quality we observe in congressional elections over this period.

Notes

1 The spending variables were logged in this analysis to normalize the distribution of spending variables. Results of models with standard spending variables available from author, by request.
2 I also create an interaction term with incumbent margin of victory and lagged incumbent spending. The results are reported in Table 8.6. The estimated value of the coefficient of this interaction term is not significant at conventional levels.

9
IMPLICATIONS
Challenger Quality, Incumbency Advantage, and Democracy in America

The preceding chapters aimed to document and explain the decline in congressional challenger quality we observe between 1972 and 2018. This chapter considers some of the implications of these developments with respect to the democratic process. Specifically, I will investigate whether the decline in challenger quality has helped to insulate incumbents from electoral vulnerability. From a normative point of view, such an effect may be detrimental because it has the potential to diminish democratic responsiveness (Tufte 1973; King and Gelman 1991). I advance this analysis by examining developments in incumbency advantage and considering the influence of declining challenger quality on the patterns we observe during the period of my study.

Incumbency Advantage

Few political phenomena have been scrutinized as closely as incumbency advantage over the past three decades. Since Erikson (1971) originally observed the growth in the electoral advantage associated with incumbency, scholars have labored extensively to monitor and to explain its substantial rise. Cox and Katz (2002: 159) count "no fewer than 145 works dealing with incumbency advantage in congressional elections" in the standard bibliography of scholarly work on Congress (Goehlert, Martin, and Sayre 1996). In fact, incumbency has been described as the "central connective thread" that connects the entire contemporary literature on Congress (Alford and Brady 1989).

Scholars have investigated incumbency advantage by measuring "sophomore surges" and "retirement slumps" (Erikson 1971; Cover and Mayhew 1977; Born 1986; Alford and Brady 1988), "vanishing marginals" (Mayhew 1974; Jacobson 1987), incumbent voteshares (Alford and Hibbing 1981), and more complex estimations (Gelman and King 1990; Cox and Katz 1996; Cain, Ferejohn, and Fiorina 1987; Erikson 1971; Carson and Roberts 2005).

Growth in the incumbency advantage that emerged in the 1960s has been explained by emphasizing incumbent resources (Mayhew 1974), including opportunities to perform constituency service (Fiorina 1977; 1989), partisan dealignment (Erikson 1971; Ferejohn 1977), fundraising advantages (Abramowitz 1991), strategic entry (Cox and Katz 1996; 2002), redistricting (Cox and Katz 2002), party machine structure (Carson and Roberts 2014) and the spread of local television news (Prior 2006).

Even early on, some scholars expressed skepticism about growth in the incumbency advantage. Jacobson (1987) noted that the size of vote swings from election to election had increased, despite increases in incumbents' electoral margins. He claimed this phenomenon had not improved incumbents' likelihood of victory. Using a different metric and calling for an adjusted methodological approach to measuring incumbents' electoral safety, Cox and Katz (2002) argued that the growth in incumbency advantage documented extensively by scholars may have simply been an artifact of biased estimation. Similarly, Stonecash (2008) argued the incumbent advantage was a statistical artifact rooted in measurement bias. He claimed the often-made choice to exclude uncontested seats from analyses had muddled the results of studies of incumbency bias (Stonecash 2008). Notwithstanding any growth in the 1960s, recent studies suggest the electoral benefits of incumbency have dwindled, at least since the mid-1980s. In fact, Jacobson (2015) finds the incumbency advantage has declined to near pre-1960s levels with the rise of party loyalty that has pushed partisan considerations [back] to the forefront of voting decisions at the expense of other advantages (resources, etc.) that incumbents may have previously enjoyed. Jacobson (2015) also argues the apparent incumbency advantage growth cited during the late 20th century had been masked by other trends, such as incumbent spending advantages (Abramowitz 1991). These developments continue to give incumbents an edge in elections, but the advantage accrued simply by being an incumbent has actually diminished (Jacobson 2015).

Given the influential role challenger quality plays in election outcomes, it is worth considering how the developments in this arena over the past half-century documented throughout this book may (or may not) be linked to patterns in incumbency advantage in elections to Congress.

Challenger Quality and Incumbency Advantage

In seeking to estimate the incumbency advantage, Cox and Katz (1996) argue that incumbency confers valuable resources and exposure that have both direct and indirect effects on the vote.

> The direct effect arises because legislative resources (e.g. personal staff) can be used in electorally useful ways (e.g. to perform casework). The

indirect effect arises because potential challengers, knowing that incumbents can derive large direct benefits from the resources at their disposal, will be less inclined to enter the fray—and this will be particularly true of potential challengers with higher opportunity costs, hence higher quality challengers.

(Cox and Katz 1996: 479).

They call this a "scare-off" effect. Cox and Katz go on to argue that, to explain overtime trends in incumbency advantage in congressional elections, "it is crucial to understand why having had previous electoral experience became more and more important in predicting voteshares" (2002: 480).

These claims suggest that developments in patterns of overall candidate quality may affect incumbency advantage in important ways. The decline in overall challenger quality between 1972 and 2018 documented in Chapter 1 may reflect that incumbents are increasingly better at "scaring off" high-quality challengers. If this is the case, declining challenger quality in congressional elections may have boosted incumbency advantage during this period by altering one of the components of the indirect effect on incumbency advantage: the scare-off effect. I investigate this possibility below.

Incumbency Advantage: Direct and Indirect Components

To investigate the impact of developments in overall challenger quality on incumbency advantage, I will follow the methodological procedures set forth by Cox and Katz (1996). Cox and Katz (1996) decompose incumbency advantage into two main parts: Direct and indirect. The indirect value of incumbency, they argue, arises as the multiplicative product of two other factors. Knowledge about incumbents' access to valuable resources scares off better-qualified, more formidable challengers (*scare off* effect) "leaving only patsies to take on most incumbents seeking reelection" (Cox and Katz 1996: 482). But this scare-off effect would not influence incumbent voteshares if the challengers' qualifications did not matter in determining the final vote tally (Cox and Katz 1996: 482–483). Thus, the second component of the indirect value of incumbency—the quality effect—measures how much candidate quality differentials affect the vote (Cox and Katz 1996).

The product of the scare-off effect (the presence of the incumbent lowers the expected quality of the challenger by X units) and the quality effect (an X unit decrement in challenger quality increases the incumbent's expected voteshare by Y) define the total indirect value of incumbency (Cox and Katz 1996: 483).

The measure of candidate quality used in the analysis is prior elective experience (Jacobson 1978; 1980), which corresponds with the measure of quality used in all the other analyses in the preceding chapters.

The Model

To measure incumbency advantage, Cox and Katz (1996) estimate the following model (Equation 1), adapted from Gelman and King (1990):

$$v_{j,t} = \delta_0 + \delta_1 v_{j,t-1} + \delta_2 P_{j,t} + \delta_3 I_{j,t-1} + \delta_4 \mathbf{DEMQA}_{j,t-1}$$
$$+ \psi_t I_{j,t} + \theta_1 \mathbf{DEMQA}_{j,t} + \varepsilon_{j,t}$$

Where,

- $v_{j,t}$ is the Democratic share of the two-party vote in district j at election t;
- $v_{j,t-1}$ is the Democratic share of the two-party vote in district j at election $t-1$;
- $P_{j,t}$ equals 1 if the Democrats are the incumbent party and -1 if the Republicans are the incumbent party in district j at election t;
- $I_{j,t}$ equals 1 if there is a Democratic incumbent, 0 if there are no incumbents and -1 if there is a republican incumbent seeking reelection in district j at election t;
- $I_{j,t-1}$ equals 1 if there is a Democratic incumbent, 0 if there are no incumbents and -1 if there is a Republican incumbent seeking reelection in district j at election $t-1$;
- $\mathbf{DEMQA}_{j,t}$ equals $+1$ if the Democratic candidate has previously held elective office but the Republican candidate has not, 0 if neither or both candidates have previously held elective office; -1 if the Republican candidate has previously held elective office while the Democratic candidate has not in district j at election t.
- $\mathbf{DEMQA}_{j,t-1}$ equals $+1$ if the Democratic candidate has previously held elective office but the Republican candidate has not, 0 if neither or both candidates have previously held elective office; -1 if the Republican candidates has previously held elective office while the Democratic candidate has not in district j at election $t-1$.
- $\varepsilon_{j,t}$ is an error term.

Based on parameters estimated for the model above, Cox and Katz (1996) explain that the value of $\hat{\psi}_t$ will reflect the *direct* benefits of incumbency. The value of the OLS estimate $\hat{\theta}_t$ will measure the *quality* effect. No parameter in Equation 1 provides an estimate of the scare-off effect. To estimate this effect, Cox and Katz (1996) regress $\mathbf{DEMQA}_{j,t}$ on a vector of regressors including $I_{j,t}$. The coefficient on $I_{j,t}$ ($\hat{\sigma}$) in this regression measures the scare-off effect. Multiplying this coefficient ($\hat{\sigma}$) by $\hat{\theta}_1$ converts this impact on quality into an impact on voteshares. This product represents the total indirect effect. The overall effect of incumbency thus, in standard path-analytic fashion, is $\hat{\psi}_t + \hat{\theta}_t + \hat{\sigma}_t$.

The model Cox and Katz develop to determine the Democratic quality advantage ($\mathbf{DEMQA}_{j,t}$) is sensitive to all the predetermined values that affect the Democratic vote, including the lagged Democratic quality advantage. Thus, Equation 2:

$$\text{DEMQA}_{j,t} = \gamma_0 + \gamma_1 \mathbf{v}_{j,t-1} + \gamma_{2t} \mathbf{P}_{j,t} + \gamma_{3t} \mathbf{I}_{j,t-1}$$
$$+ \gamma_{4t} \text{DEMQA}_{j,t-1} + \sigma_t \mathbf{I}_{j,t} + \pi_{j,t}$$

The equation is run separately for each year, excluding years that follow redistricting (King and Gelman 1991; Gelman and King 1990). (Details and elaboration about the model can be found in Cox and Katz 1996.)

Findings 1948–1990: Cox and Katz (1996)

Estimates and results for the period 1948–1990 appear in Cox and Katz (1996). The authors found evidence of growth in the incumbency advantage during this period, showing that the total effect of incumbency increased from 0.54 in 1948 to a peak of 13.11 in 1966 to 8.47 in 1990. Their analyses suggest this growth, "stems substantially, if not primarily, from growth in the indirect effect" (486). Growth in the overall direct effect was never statistically significantly different from zero. In fact, Cox and Katz found that, while the indirect effect constituted only 9.5% of the total incumbency effect in 1950, it accounted for 28.2% of the effect in 1990. Moreover, growth in the indirect effect appeared to stem primarily from growth in the quality effect. Indeed, they reported that the quality effect more than doubled from 1968 to 1976, while growth in the scare-off effect was never statistically discernible from zero.

Cox and Katz concluded that growth in incumbency advantage was fueled by the increase in the quality effect (1996). They suggest the increase in the quality effect was driven by a decline in partisanship within the electorate that heightened the importance of candidate quality as a voting cue. They also speculated that the growth in the quality effect could be explained by experienced politicians' increasingly superior campaign execution abilities relative to inexperienced candidates. They speculated further that redistricting may have accelerated the growth of the indirect effects further, a story they explored more extensively in later work (Cox and Katz 2002).

Recent Trends in Incumbency Advantage

Has the growth in incumbency advantaged been sustained? If so, have developments in the patterns of experienced candidate recruitment during this period impacted the dynamics of incumbency advantage we observe? The remainder of this chapter aims to address these questions by focusing on developments between 1974 and 2018. Using the Cox and Katz methods described above, I have estimated parameters to extend Cox and Katz's analysis by nearly three, additional decades (to 2018).[1] The estimates are presented in Table 9.1.[2] The overall

TABLE 9.1 Decomposition of Incumbency Advantage in U.S. House Elections (1974–2018)

	Type of Effect [1]					
	Direct Effect	Quality Effect	Scare-Off Effect	Indirect Effect	Total	(%) Total
1974	3.46 (1.37)	4.55 (0.87)	0.49 (0.08)	2.21	5.67	0.39
1976	5.67 (1.36)	4.81 (0.83)	0.37 (0.09)	1.8	7.46	0.24
1978	9.36 (1.49)	5.6 (1.06)	0.4 (0.08)	2.25	11.61	0.19
1980	5.76 (1.6)	3.34 (1.03)	0.37 (0.08)	1.23	6.99	0.18
1984	8.28 (1.58)	3.67 (0.9)	0.33 (0.09)	1.22	9.5	0.13
1986	9.41 (1.23)	5.42 (0.84)	0.52 (0.08)	2.82	12.23	0.23
1988	9.32 (1.57)	2.57 (0.89)	0.61 (0.09)	1.56	10.89	0.14
1990	6.23 (1.62)	2.99 (1.04)	0.63 (0.08)	1.88	8.11	0.23
1994	7.54 (1.15)	4.72 (0.84)	0.48 (0.07)	2.27	9.81	0.23
1996	4.44 (1)	3 (0.73)	0.31 (0.07)	0.93	5.37	0.17
1998	6.47 (1.05)	3.39 (0.67)	0.49 (0.08)	1.65	8.11	0.2
2000	7.73 (1.41)	2.67 (0.76)	0.74 (0.1)	1.97	9.69	0.2
2004	6.16 (1.13)	3.42 (0.72)	0.07 (0.09)	0.24	6.4	0.04
2006	6.03 (1.09)	3.94 (0.72)	0.28 (0.09)	1.09	7.12	0.15
2008	4.94 (1.04)	4.13 (0.7)	0.52 (0.08)	2.16	7.1	0.3
2010	2.91 (1.1)	3.29 (0.67)	0.45 (0.09)	1.48	4.4	0.34
2014	2.76 (0.8)	0.83 (0.55)	0.44 (0.08)	0.37	3.13	0.12
2016	0.77 (0.96)	1.96 (0.6)	0.52 (0.09)	1.02	1.79	0.57
2018	2.14 (0.66)	0.81 (0.52)	0.35 (0.07)	0.29	2.43	0.12

[1] 1974-2018 data compiled by author. Standard errors in parentheses where applicable. Redistricting years excluded from analysis (1972, 1982, 1992, 2002, 2012).

---

incumbency effect (direct plus indirect effects) that appears in column 6 of the table is displayed visually in Figure 9.1. An analysis of the data suggests that we observe a statistically significant erosion in the vote-denominated incumbency advantage when the time series is restricted to this period. The estimated slope of the coefficient from a regression of the total effect on a constant and a time trend suggests an average decrease of 0.27 (standard error = 0.07) percentage points per year ($p < 0.01$). It appears that incumbents' electoral advantage has stopped climbing and has been trending downward, at least between 1974 and 2018, a finding that is broadly consistent with claims advanced in Jacobson (2015).

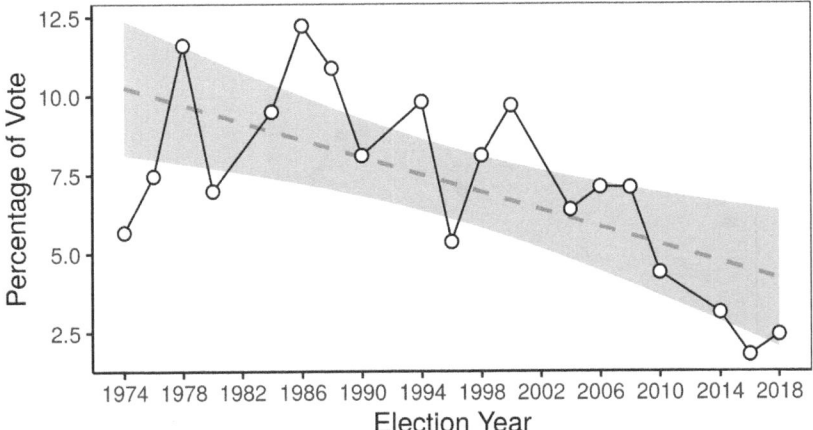

[1] Dashed line indicates OLS regression line of best fit over time trend.

FIGURE 9.1 Estimates of Total Incumbency Advantage in U.S. House Elections (1974–2018)[1]

To zoom in on the role of candidate quality in these developments, Table 9.1 also decomposes the incumbency advantage into its direct and indirect effect components, as described above, for the period 1974–2018. The data is presented visually in Figure 9.2 and analyzed in Table 9.2. The data confirm several of Cox and Katz's (1996) initial findings. The direct effects of incumbency (resources, etc.) remain dominant, exceeding the total indirect effects substantially in every election cycle. Yet the overall indirect effects continue to contribute anywhere from a 0.24 to 2.82 percentage point advantage to incumbents over this period. On average, indirect effects represent about a fifth (22%) of the total incumbency advantage.

The analysis presented in Table 9.2 confirms no growth in the effect of direct advantages to incumbents; in fact, there is a statistically significant *decline* in the direct effect (coefficient = -0.22, $p < 0.01$). When the analysis is limited to this period, however, several patterns that differ from the original (Cox and Katz 1996) study appear. While Cox and Katz (1996) observed a statistically significant growth in the impact of indirect effects (at least between 1956 and 1983) in their study, no such trend is sustained between 1974 and 2018. In fact, the overall impact of indirect effects is on the decline (–0.06), and is statistically significant ($p < 0.01$).

Moreover, the consistent growth in the quality effect documented by Cox and Katz also disappears over this period. Indeed, the quality effect also seems to be on the decline (–0.13), and is also statistically significant ($p < 0.01$). This implies that any advantages to incumbents of being contested by inexperienced (low-quality) challengers, while still positive, have diminished. While quality

116 Implications

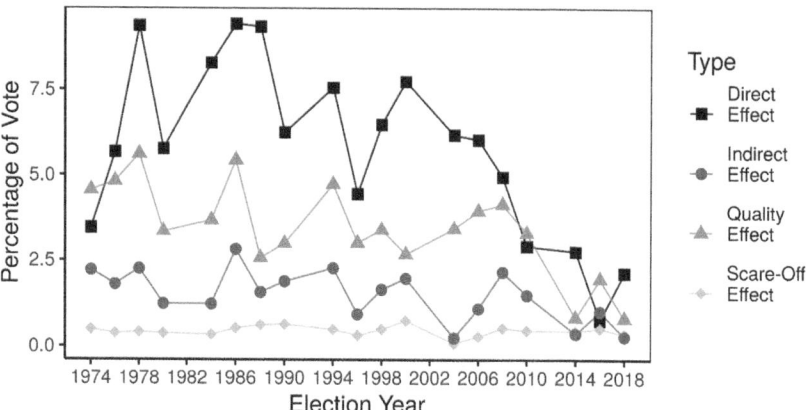

FIGURE 9.2 Direct and Indirect Effects (Scare-off and Quality) in House Elections (1974–2018)

TABLE 9.2 Rate of Growth in Direct and Indirect Effects in House Elections (1974–2018)[1]

	Direct Effect	Indirect Effect	Quality Effect	Scare-Off Effect
Coefficient [2] (Std. Error)	-0.215** (0.071)	-0.06** (0.021)	-0.13** (0.033)	-0.001 (0.005)

[1] Values represent OLS coefficients on values indicated in Table 9.1 for each category of effect regressed on time and a constant.

[2] *** $p < 0.001$, ** $p < 0.01$, * $p < 0.05$, . $p < 0.10$.

advantages boosted incumbents' voteshares by about 4 percentage points on average in the 1970s and 1980s, quality effects have bumped incumbent support by 2–3 percentage points on average in elections since 2000. The scare-off effect, on average, is declining modestly, but the drop does not approach statistical significance at conventional levels. Consistent with Cox and Katz (1996), the analysis suggests no overall growth in the scare-off effect between 1974 and 2018.

Why Has the Quality Effect Declined?

Cox and Katz (1996) offer two explanations for the increase in the quality effect they observe between the mid-1950s and the mid-1980s. They argue that the growth in quality effect resulted from declining partisanship in the electorate (which caused candidates' personal characteristics to matter more in elections) and the ability of high-quality candidates to manage campaigns more effectively, especially after court-mandated redistrictings disrupted districts and attenuated local party organizations' electioneering capacity.

Developments in each of these two areas may help explain why the quality effect has reversed its upward trend between 1974 and 2018. First, recent studies find that partisanship in the electorate has stopped its downward spiral and provide evidence that partisanship is increasingly more potent. Bartels (2000) argues that the conventional wisdom regarding party decline is exaggerated and outdated. In fact, he finds that "partisan loyalties in the American public have rebounded significantly since the mid-1970s" (2000: 35). Jacobson (2015) generally concurs with this assessment, noting that growing nationalization in congressional elections has shifted the emphasis of voting choices back to partisan orientations (and away from incumbent resources or even candidate qualities). Second, the tremendous growth in the political consulting industry provides access to effective campaign management, even to less experienced candidates who increasingly run professionalized campaigns (Thurber and Nelson 2000; Herrnson 1995). Combined, these developments may help to explain why the quality effect is on the decline.

Discussion

Incumbency advantage appears to have stopped growing in U.S. elections because both its direct and indirect components have stopped growing. In fact, both direct and indirect effects, along with the scare-off and quality dimensions, appear to be declining over the past half-century or so, as is incumbency advantage overall. The steepest decline I observe over the period I examine relates to the direct effect. Access to the resources and visibility that advantaged incumbents in the past seem to be less and less influential in boosting incumbent voteshares on Election Day. Despite declining challenger quality levels in congressional elections, my findings suggest the scare-off effect has not changed much since the 1970s (if anything, it also appears to be eroding, but at a much slower pace than other components). The analyses also suggest the indirect effect comprises a larger share of the overall (total) incumbency advantage in recent cycles, accounting for between 12 and 57 percent of the total advantage in the four most recent elections included in the analysis.

Conclusion

Some scholars believe incumbency advantage may threaten the fundamental character of representative democracy in America. Incumbents isolated from electoral swings are likely to be less attentive to their constituencies, resulting in a system that is considerably less responsive (Mayhew 1974; Fiorina 1977; Brady 1988). Indeed, Gelman and King (1990) find evidence of declining responsiveness and attribute this decline partly to incumbency advantage.

The results of the analyses in this chapter suggest the growth in incumbency advantage has leveled off and is trending downward, thus assuaging at least some concerns about further declining responsiveness. These findings mirror other recent work on the subject and provide more evidence that the incumbency effect has diminished (Jacobson 2015). Notwithstanding declining rates of challenger quality in congressional elections overall since the 1970s, it may be comforting to note that incumbents' ability to thwart formidable challenges has not strengthened over this period (and may have even eroded somewhat), potentially counteracting other developments that weakened incumbency advantage. By itself, this phenomenon represents an important development. It may also be encouraging that, while fewer and fewer experienced challengers are emerging to contest congressional incumbents since the 1970s, incumbents cannot rely as much as in the past on any advantages afforded by facing inexperienced challengers. Although experienced challengers continue to outperform their inexperienced counterparts in congressional races against incumbents, even low-quality challengers can seemingly put up decent fights in recent election cycles, cutting into incumbents' support at the polls by wider and wider margins than in previous periods.

Notes

1 I acknowledge that my replications yield estimates that differ somewhat from those reported in Cox and Katz (1996) for comparable years, but both sets of measures are generally strongly correlated: direct effect (.96); scare-off effect (.95); quality effect (.50); indirect effect (.34).
2 Consistent with previous work (Cox and Katz 1996; Gelman and King 1990), the analysis excludes cycles that follow redistrictings, thus starting in 1974. Data from 1974–1990 appear in Cox and Katz 1996. Data from 1990–2018 are compiled by the author.

10
CONCLUSION

Challenger quality is an important determinant of electoral outcomes in congressional elections in the United States (Jacobson 1992). As such, over time developments in the frequency of experienced challengers that we observe in contested congressional elections represent an important—and often neglected—area of inquiry for students of congressional elections. The objective of this book is to help fill part of that void, to reflect on patterns we observe over time, and to speculate about explanations that help to account for these developments.

What Have We Learned?

This book contributes the following main insights to the literature on congressional elections.

1. *Overall challenger quality declined between 1972 and 2018.*

Despite the relative simplicity of this finding, few other studies have focused on general patterns in challenger quality over time. This book documents and describes in detail the magnitude of the decline in quality we observe between 1972 and 2018. I show that the proportion of quality challengers, defined as those with prior experience in elective office, has declined by an average of 0.4 percentage points in each of the 24 election cycles included in this study. I also show both parties have increasingly failed to recruit experienced challengers during this period, but that the decline among Democratic challengers has been more pronounced.

2. *Declining competitiveness explains virtually all of the overall decline in quality observed during this period.*

This was one of three main explanations I considered for the decline in quality observed between 1972 and 2018. I hypothesized that quality challengers may be discouraged from declining competitiveness. I showed that competitiveness, defined as the incumbent's party's electoral strength in the district, has indeed declined over this period, and the analyses I conducted confirm that declining competitiveness accounts for nearly all of the overall decline in quality I observe.

3. *Escalating campaign costs do not explain the decline in challenger quality.*

I also consider another possible explanation for the decline in quality: Escalating campaign costs. I confirm that campaign costs have indeed risen substantially between 1972 and 2018. The empirical analyses I conduct do not provide evidence that campaign costs depress challenger quality. In fact, if there is any effect increased spending appears to increase challenger quality. Therefore, I dismiss this as a possible alternative explanation for the decline in quality.

4. *The adoption and implementation of state legislative term limits legislation has not contributed to the decline in challenger quality.*

I develop and test hypotheses about the effect of state legislative term limits on challenger quality. I describe the institutionalization of state legislative term limits in various states across the country in detail, but I find no consistent empirical evidence that state legislative term limits depress challenger quality. As such, I also dismiss state legislative term limits as an alternative explanation for declining challenger quality.

5. *Despite declining levels of challenger quality, incumbency advantage has declined since the 1970s.*

In tandem with other developments, declining rates of experienced challengers in congressional elections since the 1970s do not appear to have been sufficient to strengthen incumbency advantage. In fact, I find incumbency advantage has declined significantly over the period of my study, a result that reinforces extant scholarship on the topic (Jacobson 2015). Incumbents seemingly benefit no more from discouraging strong opposition now than in the past. And while incumbents continue to benefit from facing inexperienced challengers, compared to their experienced counterparts, such advantages at the ballot box appear to be eroding, potentially assuaging concerns about the implications of declining challenger quality on democratic responsiveness. Challenger experience remains an important influence on election outcomes, but quality differentials matter less than in the past for incumbency advantage. Incumbents increasingly underestimate inexperienced challengers at their peril.

Normative Implications

I began this book by reflecting on the importance of meaningful electoral contests for a system based on democratic principles. Such contests are most likely when both contenders are strong and well-financed, or, for lack of better terminology, high-quality. Imbalanced contests that pit an incumbent against an underdog do not, in my view, fare well for democracy. It is unclear why, in a nation with over 500,000 elected officials, all of whom would be considered high-quality by the standard of prior electoral experienced adopted in this (and in most) studies, and with a plethora of experienced politicians assumed to possess ambition to move onward to higher elective office, so few contests against incumbents include experienced challengers. It is even more troubling for democracy that the trend appears to be fewer such challengers over time.

Public policy measures to promote more meaningful electoral contests implicitly, if not always explicitly, aim to achieve this goal. Certainly, this is an outcome that would appeal to proponents of state legislative term limits or publicly financed campaigns. According to my analyses, however, such measures are unlikely to promote more meaningful electoral contests by pitting two strong opponents against each other.

A more productive way to increase the presence of high-quality challengers in races against incumbents would be to introduce mechanisms that increase the competitiveness of congressional districts, defined by the district's partisan profile. Leveraging the redistricting process to accomplish this may be one institutional solution. Another option would be to leverage the political party system. Even as some scholars have argued that political party strength has waned in American society (Wattenberg 1990), giving rise to the candidate-centered politics and campaigns (Wattenberg 1991), parties may still tap more aggressively into their role in candidate recruitment to encourage and support high-quality challengers to contest incumbents. After all, the failure of the minority party to field viable congressional challengers in a district may solidify or enhance the majority party's superiority in the district. Conceding these races to the majority party will not help prospects for the minority party in the district. Meaningful contests for Congress, on the other hand, between two viable contenders from opposing parties may help districts to achieve (or maintain) a competitive partisan balance in the district. Politically imbalanced districts in which one party or another dominates the electoral context will not attract formidable opposition against incumbents, even when such candidates are abundant.

Critics may argue that declining challenger quality is not problematic for democracy. After all, perhaps incumbents serve their districts sufficiently well, and experienced contenders are simply being strategic, waiting for promising conditions before tossing their hats into the ring. Moreover, as the partisan affiliation of districts' congressional representatives increasingly reflects the ideological composition of the electorates they represent, why should we be concerned about weak opposition from the alternative party? These claims notwithstanding, the phenomenon of declining quality in congressional races against incumbents represents, at the very least, enough of a potential threat to democratic responsiveness to merit scholarly attention, examination, and monitoring.

REFERENCES

Abramowitz, Alan. 1984. "National Issues, Strategic Politicians and Voting Behavior in the 1980 and 1982 Congressional Elections." *American Journal of Political Science 18*: 710–721.
Abramowitz, Alan. 1988. "Explaining Senate Election Outcomes." *American Political Science Review 82*: 385–403.
Abramowitz, Alan. 1989. "Campaign Spending in U.S. Senate Elections." *Legislative Studies Quarterly 14*: 487–507.
Abramowitz, Alan I. 1991. "Incumbency, Campaign Spending, and the Decline of Competition in U.S. House Elections." *Journal of Politics 53*: 34–56.
Abramowitz, Alan, Brad Alexander and Matthew Gunning. 2005. "Incumbency, Redistricting and the Decline of Competition in U.S. House Elections." Paper presented at the Annual Meeting of the Southern Political Association. New Orleans, LA. January 6–8.
Abramsom, P., J. Aldrich and D.W. Rhode. 1987. "Progressive Ambition among United States Senators: 1972–1988." *Journal of Politics 49*: 3–35.
Abramsom, P., J. Aldrich and D.W. Rhode. 1999. *Change and Continuity in the 1996 and 1998 Elections*. Washington, DC: Congressional Quarterly.
Abramowitz, Alan and Jeffrey A. Segal. 1992. *Senate Elections*. University of Michigan Press.
Adams, Greg and Peverill Squire. 1997. "Incumbent Vulnerability and Challenger Emergence in Senate Elections." *Political Behavior 19*(2): 97–111.
Aldrich, John. 1995. *Why Parties? The Origin and Transformation of Political Parties in America*. Chicago, IL: University of Chicago Press.
Alford, J. and J. Hibbing. 1981. "Increased Incumbency Advantage in the House." *Journal of Politics 41*: 1042–1061.
Alford, John R. and David W. Brady. 1989. "Personal and Partisan Advantage in U.S. Congressional Elections." In eds. Lawrence C. Dodd and Bruce I. Oppenhemier. *Congress Reconsidered*. 4th ed. Praeger Publishers.
Ansolabehere, S. and J.M. Snyder. 2000. "Money and Office: The Source of Incumbency Advantage in Congressional Campaign Finance." In eds. Brady, D., J. Cogan and M. Fiorina. *Continuity and Change in House Elections*. Stanford, CA: Stanford University Press.

Ansolabehere, Stephen and Alan Gerber. 1997. "Incumbency Advantage and the Persistence of Legislative Majorities." *Legislative Studies Quarterly* 22: 161–178.

Arceneaux, K., J. Dunaway, M. Johnson and R. J. V. Wielen. 2020. "Strategic Candidate Entry and Congressional Elections in the Era of Fox News." *American Journal of Political Science* 64(2): 398–415.

Arnold, C. Benjamin and Larycia Hawkins. 2002. "Candidate Quality Properly Understood." Paper presented at the Annual Meeting of the American Political Science Association, August 29–September 1, 2002, Boston, MA.

Baker, Ross K. 1995. *House and Senate*. 2nd ed. New York: W.W. Norton.

Bartels, L. M. 2000. "Partisanship and Voting Behavior, 1952–1996." *American Journal of Political Science* 44(1): 35–50.

Banks, J. and D.R. Kiewiet. 1989. "Explaining Patterns of Candidate Competition in Congressional Elections." *American Journal of Political Science* 33: 997–1015.

Barnes, Tiffany D., Regina P. Branton and Erin C. Cassese. 2017. "A Reexamination of Women's Electoral Success in Open Seat Elections: The Conditioning Effect of Electoral Competition." *Journal of Women, Politics & Policy* 38: 298–317.

Bianco, William T. 1984. "Strategic Decisions on Candidacy in U.S. Congressional Districts." *Legislative Studies Quarterly* 9: 351–364.

Biersack, Robert, Paul Herrnson and Clyde Wilcox. 1993. "Seeds for Success: Early Money in Congressional Elections." *Legislative Studies Quarterly* 18: 535–551.

Black, Gordon. 1972. "A Theory of Political Ambition: Career Choices and the Role of Structural Incentives." *American Political Science Review* 66: 144–159.

Bond, J., G. Covington and R. Fleisher. 1985. "Explaining Challenger Quality in Congressional Elections." *Journal of Politics* 47: 510–529.

Bond, J. R., R. Fleisher and J. C. Talbert. 1997. "Partisan Differences in Candidate Quality in Open Seat House Races, 1976–1994." *Political Research Quarterly* 50(2): 281–299.

Born, Richard. 1986. "Strategic Politicians and Unresponsive Voters." *American Political Science Review* 80: 599–612.

Brace, Paul. 1984. "Progressive Ambition in the House: A Probabilistic Approach." *Journal of Politics* 46: 556–571.

Brady, D., J. Cogan and M. Fiorina. 2000. *Continuity and Change in House Elections*. Stanford: Stanford University Press.

Brady, David, Robert D'Onofrio and Morris Fiorina. 2000. "The Nationalization of Electoral Forces Revisited." In eds. Brady, D., J. Cogan and M. Fiorina. *Continuity and Change in House Elections*. Stanford: Stanford University Press.

Brambor, Thomas, William Clark and Matthew Golder. 2006. "Understanding Interaction Models: Improving Empirical Analyses." *Political Analysis* 14: 63–82.

Braumoeller, Bear F. 2004. "Hypothesis Testing and Multiplicative Interactive Terms." *International Organizations*. 58: 807–820.

Buttice, Matthew K. and Walter J. Stone. 2012. "Candidates Matter: Policy and Quality Differences in Congressional Elections." *The Journal of Politics* 74: 870–887.

Cain, Bruce. 1984. *The Reapportionment Puzzle*. Berkeley, CA: University of California Press.

Cain, Bruce, John Ferejohn and Morris Fiorina. 1987. *The Personal Vote*. Cambridge: Harvard University Press.

Canon, David T. 1990. *Actors, Athletes and Astronauts: Political Amateurs in the United States Congress*. Chicago, IL: Chicago University Press.

Carson, Jamie and Jason Roberts. 2005. "Strategic Politicians and U.S. House Elections 1874–1914." *Journal of Politics* 67: 474–496.

Carson, Jamie L. 2005. "Strategy, Selection, and Candidate Competition in U.S. House and Senate Elections." *The Journal of Politics* 67(1): 1–28.

Carson, Jamie, M.H. Crespin, C.P. Eaves and E. Wanless 2011. "Constituency Congruency and Candidate Competition in U.S. House Elections." *Legislative Studies Quarterly* 36(3): 461–482.

Carson, Jamie and Jason Roberts. 2014. *Ambition, Competition, and Electoral Reform: The Politics of Congressional Elections Across Time*. Ann Arbor, MI: The University of Michigan Press.

Choirat, Christine, James Honaker, Kosuke Imai, Gary King and Olivia Lau. 2017. Zelig: Everyone's Statistical Software. Version 5.1-3. Available at http://zeligproject.org/

Cover, Albert. 1977. "One Good Term Deserves Another: The Advantage of Incumbency in Congressional Elections." *American Journal of Political Science* 21: 523–541.

Cox, Gary W. and Jonathan N. Katz. 1996. "Why Did Incumbency Advantage in U.S. House Elections Grow?" *American Journal of Political Science* 40: 478–497.

Cox, Gary W. and Jonathan N. Katz. 2002. *Elbridge Gerry's Salamander: The Electoral Consequences of the Reapportionment Revolution*. New York: Cambridge University Press.

Davidson, Roger H. and Walter J. Oleszek. 2004. *Congress & Its Members*. 9th ed. Washington, DC: CQ Press.

Desmarais, Bruce A., Raymond J. La Raja and Michael S. Kowl. 2014. "The Fates of Challengers in U.S. House Elections: The Role of Extended Party Networks in Supporting Candidates and Shaping Electoral Outcomes." *American Journal of Political Science* 59: 194–211.

DiClerico, Robert E. 2000. *Political Parties, Campaigns and Elections*. Saddle River, NJ: Prentice Hall.

Epstein, D. and P. Zemsky. 1995. "Money Talks: Deterring Quality Challengers in Congressional Elections." *American Political Science Review* 89: 295–308.

Erikson, Robert S. 1971. "The Advantage of Incumbency in Congressional Elections." *Polity* 3: 395–405.

Farmer, Rick, John David Rausch Jr. and John C. Green. 2003. *The Test of Time: Coping With Legislative State legislative term limits*. Lanham, MD: Lexington Books.

Ferejohn, John. 1977. "On the Decline of Competition in Congressional Elections." *American Political Science Review* 71: 166–176.

Fiorina, Morris P. 1977. "The Case of the Vanishing Marginals: The Bureaucracy Did It." *American Political Science Review* 7: 177–181.

Fiorina, Morris P. 1989. *Congress: Keystone of the Washington Establishment*. 2nd ed. New Haven, CT: Yale University Press.

Fowler, Linda. 1979. "The Electoral Lottery: The Decision to Run." *Public Choice* 34: 399–418.

Fowler, Linda. 1993. *Candidates, Congress and the American Democracy*. Ann Arbor, MI: University of Michigan Press.

Fowler, Linda and Robert D. McClure. 1989. *Political Ambition: Who Decides to Run for Congress?* New Haven, CT: Yale University Press.

Francis, Wayne L. and Lawrence W. Kenney. 1997. "Equilibrium Projections of the Consequences of State legislative term limits upon Expected Tenure, Institutional Turnover, and Membership Experience." *Journal of Politics* 59: 240–252.

Friedrich, Robert. 1982. "In Defense of Multiplicative Terms in Multiple Regression Equations." *American Journal of Political Science* 26(4): 797–833.

Gaddie, Ronald Keith and Charles S. Bullock. 2000. *Elections to Open Seats in the U.S. House: Where the Action Is*. Lanham, MD: Rowman & Littlefield.

Gelman, Andrew and Gary King. 1990. "Estimating Incumbency Advantage without Bias." *American Journal of Political Science* 34(4): 1142–1164.

Goehlert, R., F. S. Martin and J. R. Sayre. 1996. *"Members of Congress : A Bibliography / Robert U. Goehlert, Fenton S. Martin, John R. Sayre."* Congressional Quarterly.

Goldstein, K and P. Freedman. 2000. "New Evidence for New Arguments: Money and Advertising in the 1996 Senate Elections." *Journal of Politics* 62: 1087–1108.

Gray, Virginia and Russell Hanson. 2004. *Politics in the American States: A Comparative Analysis.* 8th ed. Washington, DC: CQ Press.

Green, Donald and Jonathan S. Krasno. 1988. "Salvation for the Spendthrift Incumbent: Reestimating the Effects of Campaign Spending in House Elections." *American Journal of Political Science* 32: 884–907.

Grofman, Bernard. (ed.) 1996. *Legislative State Legislative Term Limits: Public Choice Perspectives.* Boston, MA: Kluwer Publishers.

Gronke, Paul. 2001. *The Electorate, the Campaign and the Office: A Unified Approach to Senate and House Elections.* Ann Arbor, MI: University of Michigan Press.

Herrnson, Paul. 1995. *Congressional Elections: Campaigning at Home and in Washington.* Washington, DC: CQ Press.

Imai, Kosuke, Gary King and Olivia Lau. 2008. "Toward A Common Framework for Statistical Analysis and Development." *Journal of Computational Graphics and Statistics.* 17: 892–913.

Jacobson, Gary C. 1978. "The Effects of Campaign Spending in Congressional Elections." *American Political Science Review* 72: 469–491.

Jacobson, Gary C. 1980. *Money in Congressional Elections.* New Haven, CT: Yale University Press.

Jacobson, Gary C. 1987. "The Marginals Never Vanished: Incumbency and Competition in Elections to the U.S. House of Representatives, 1952–1982." *American Journal of Political Science* 31: 126–141.

Jacobson, Gary C. 1989. "Strategic Politicians and the Dynamics of U.S. House Elections 1946-86." *Amercian Politican Science Review* 83: 773–793.

Jacobson, Gary C. 1990. *The Electoral Origins of Divided Government: Competition in U.S. House Elections, 1946–1988.* Boulder, CO: Westview Press.

Jacobson, Gary C. 1992. *The Politics of Congressional Elections.* 3rd ed. New York: Harper Collins.

Jacobson, Gary C. 2000. "Party Polarization in National Politics: The Electoral Connection." In eds. J. Bond and R. Fleisher. *Polarized Politics: Congress and the President in a Partisan Era.* Washington, DC: Congressional Quarterly Press.

Jacobson, Gary C. 2001. *The Politics of Congressional Elections.* 5th ed. Longman.

Jacobson, Gary C. 2009. "Measuring Campaign Spending Effects in U.S. House Elections." In eds. H. Brady and R. Johnson. *Capturing Campaign Effects.* Ann Arbor, MI: University of Michigan Press.

Jacobson, Gary C. 2015. "It's Nothing Personal: The Decline of the Incumbency Advantage in US House Elections." *The Journal of Politics* 77(3): 861–873.

Jacobson, Gary C. and S. Kernell. 1981. *Strategy and Choice in Congressional Elections.* New Haven, CT: Yale University Press.

Jacobson, Gary C. and Jamie Carson 2016. *The Politics of Congressional Elections.* 9th ed. Lanham, MD: Rowman and Littlefield.

Kazee, Thomas A. 1994. *Who Runs for Congress: Ambition, Context and Candidate Emergence.* Washington, DC: CQ Press.

Key, V. O. 1949. *Southern Politics in State and Nation.* Knopf.

King, Gary and Andrew Gelman. 1991. "Systemic Consequences of Incumbency Advantage in the U. S. House." *American Journal of Political Science* 35: 110–138.

King, Gary, Michael Tomz and Jason Wittenberg. 2000. "Making the Most of Statistical Analyses: Improving Interpretation and Presentation." *American Journal of Political Science* 44(2): 347–361.

King, Gary and Andrew Gelman. 1991. "Systematic Consequences of Incumbency Advantage in U.S. House Elections." *American Journal of Political Science* 35: 110–138.

Krasno, Jonathan. 1994. *Challengers, Competition and Reelection: Comparing Senate and House Elections.* New Haven, CT: Yale University Press.

Krasno, Jonathan and Donald Green. 1988. "Preempting Quality Challengers in House Elections." *Journal of Politics* 50: 920–936.

Krasno, Jonathan and Daniel Seltz. 2000. *Buying Time: Television Advertising in the 1998 Congressional Elections.* Brennan Center for Justice and NYU School of Law.

Levine, Martin D. and Mark S. Hyde. 1977. "Incumbency and the Theory of Political Ambition: A Rational Choice Model." *Journal of Politics* 39: 959–983.

Lublin, David Ian. 1994. "Quality, Not Quantity: Strategic Politicians in U.S. Senate Elections, 1952–1990." *Journal of Politics* 56(1): 228–241.

Magleby, David B. (ed.) 2002. *Financing the 2000 Election.* Washington, DC: Brookings Institution Press.

Maisel, L., Walter Stone Sandy and Cherie Maestas (2001). "Quality Challengers to Congressional Incumbents: Can Better Candidates Be Found?" In ed. Paul Herrnson. *Playing Hardball: Campaigning for the U.S. Congress.* New Jersey: Prentice Hall.

Mayhew, David R. 1971. "Congressional Representation: Theory and Practice in Drawing the Districts." In ed. Nelson W. Polsby. *Reapportionment in the 1970s.* Berkeley, CA: University of California Press.

Mayhew, David R. 1974. *The Electoral Connection.* New Haven, CT: Yale University Press.

Nagler, Jonathan. 1991. "The Effect of Registration Laws and Education on U.S. Voter Turnout." *American Political Science Review* 85(4): 1393–1405.

Nagler, Jonathan. 1995. "Coding Style and Good Computing Practices." *PS: Political Science and Politics* 28(3): 488–492.

Owen, Guillermo and Bernard Grofman. 1988. "Optimal Partisan Gerrymandering." *Political Geography Quarterly* 7: 5–22.

Panagopoulos, C. 2017. *Political Campaigns: Concepts, Context, and Consequences.* Oxford University Press.

Petracca, Mark. 1996. "A Legislature in Transition: The California Experience With State legislative term limits." Paper presented at the annual meeting of the American Political Science Association, San Francisco.

Praino, Rodrigo, Daniel Stockemer and Vincent G. Moscardelli. 2013. "The Lingering Effect of Scandals in Congressional Elections: Incumbents, Challengers, and Voters." *Social Science Quarterly* 94: 1043–1061.

Prior, Markus. 2001. "Weighted Content Analysis of Political Advertisements." *Political Communication* 18(3): 335–345.

Prior, Marcus. 2006. "The Incumbent in the Living Room: The Rise of Television and the Incumbency Advantage in U. S. House Elections." *Journal of Politics* 68: 657–673.

Powell, Richard. 2000. "The Impact of State legislative term limits on the Candidacy Decisions of State Legislators in U.S. House Elections." *Legislative Studies Quarterly* 25(4): 645–661.

Powell, Richard. 2003. "The Unintended Effects of Term Limits on the Career Paths of State Legislators." In: eds. Farmer, Rick., John David Rausch, Jr. and John C. Green *The Test of Time: Coping with Legislative Term Limits.* Lanham MD: Lexington Books.

Pyeatt, Nicholas L. 2014. "Incumbent Ideology, District Ideology, and Candidate Entry in U.S. Congressional Elections, 1954–2008." *The Social Science Journal* 51(2): 181–190.

Ragsdale, Lyn and Timothy E. Cook. 1987. "Representatives' Actions and Challengers' Reactions: Limits to Candidate Connections in the House." *American Journal of Political Science 31*: 45–81.

Ranney, Austin. 1976. "Parties in State Politics." In eds. Herbert Jacob and Kenneth Vines. *Politics in the American States: A Comparative Analysis*. 3rd ed. Boston, MA: Little Brown.

Rhode, David. 1979. "Risk-bearing and Progressive Ambition: The Case of the U.S. House of Representatives." *American Journal of Political Science 23*(1): 1–26.

Riker, W. and P. Ordeshook. 1973. *An Introduction to Formal Political Theory*. New York: Prentice-Hall.

Schlesigner, Joseph. 1966. *Ambition and Politics: Political Careers in the United States*. Chicago, IL: Rand McNally.

Serra, G. and D. Moon. 1994. "Casework, Issue Positions and Voting in Congressional Elections: A District Analysis." *The Journal of Politics 56*: 200–213.

Sparks, Steven. 2020. "Quality Challenger Emergence under the Top-two Primary: Comparing One-party and Two-party General Election Contests." *Electoral Studies 65*: 102136.

Squire, Peverill. 1988. "Career Opportunities and Membership Stability in Legislatures." *Legislative Studies Quarterly 13*: 65–82.

Squire, Peverill. 1989. "Challengers in U.S. Senate Elections." *Legislative Studies Quarterly 14*(4): 531–547.

Squire, Peverill. 1992. "Challenger Quality and Voting Behavior in U.S. Senate Elections." *Legislative Studies Quarterly 17*(2): 247–263.

Squire, Peverill. 1995. "Candidates, Money and Voters: Assessing the State of Congressional Elections Research." *Political Research Quarterly 48*: 891–917.

Stonecash, J.M. 2008. *Reassessing the Incumbency Effect*. Cambridge: Cambridge University Press.

Thurber, James and Candice Nelson. 2000. *Campaign Warriors: Political Consultants in Elections*. Washington, DC: Brookings Institution Press.

Tomz, Michael, Jason Wittenberg and Gary King. 2003. CLARIFY: Software for Interpreting and Presenting Statistical Results. Version 2.1. Stanford University, University of Wisconsin and Harvard University. January 5. Available at http://gking.harvard.edu/.

Tufte, Edward R. 1973. "The Relationship Between Seats and Votes in Two-Party Systems." *American Political Science Review 67*: 540–554.

Van Dunk, Emily 1997. "Challenger Quality in State Legislative Election." *Political Research Quarterly 50*(4): 793–807.

Wattenberg, Martin. 1990. *The Decline of American Political Parties, 1952–1988*. Cambridge, MA: Harvard University Press.

Wattenberg, Martin. 1991. *The Rise of Candidate-Centered Politics*. Cambridge, MA: Harvard University Press.

West, D. M. 1994. "Television Advertising in Election Campaigns." *Political Science Quarterly 109*(5): 789–809. https://doi.org/10.2307/2152532.

APPENDIX

TABLE A7.1 Proportion of High-Quality Challengers (Avg., 1972–2018) and Change in Overall Proportion of High-Quality Challengers (1972–2018) by State

State	Experienced Challengers (%) 1972-2018	Change 1972-2018 °	State	Experienced Challengers (%) 1972-2018	Change 1972-2018 °
Alabama	20	-1.19 (0.63)	Montana	44	-0.86 (1.6)
Alaska	50	-1.74 (1.49)	Nebraska	24	0.4 (0.62)
Arizona	15	-0.32 (0.46)	Nevada	43	-0.88 (1.29)
Arkansas	32	2.63* (1.13)	New Hampshire	54	0.83 (1.32)
California	11	-0.15 (0.17)	New Jersey	29	-1.15** (0.39)
Colorado	37	-0.37 (0.73)	New Mexico	51	-0.93 (1.12)
Connecticut	37	0.54 (0.43)	New York	19	-0.17 (0.3)
Delaware	16	-2.86* (1.17)	North Carolina	24	-0.95* (0.42)
Florida	14	0.3 (0.23)	North Dakota	40	0.16 (1.74)
Georgia	13	-0.09 (0.38)	Ohio	22	-0.31 (0.28)
Hawaii	17	0.02 (1.07)	Oklahoma	21	-0.4 (0.59)
Idaho	38	-1.15 (1.31)	Oregon	22	-0.98 (0.58)
Illinois	12	0.27 (0.27)	Pennsylvania	16	0.09 (0.32)
Indiana	22	-1.2** (0.39)	Rhode Island	17	0.3 (0.96)
Iowa	35	-1.05 (0.58)	South Carolina	19	-1.13* (0.53)
Kansas	27	-0.44 (0.8)	South Dakota	43	-0.06 (1.61)
Kentucky	26	-0.52 (0.73)	Tennessee	10	-1.14* (0.55)
Louisiana	25	-0.62 (1.16)	Texas	10	-0.31 (0.26)
Maine	61	-0.35 (1.13)	Utah	33	-0.94 (1.1)
Maryland	21	-1.37* (0.55)	Vermont	40	-3.78* (1.54)
Massachusetts	16	-1.39* (0.61)	Virginia	28	-2.49*** (0.57)
Michigan	20	-0.33 (0.35)	Washington	23	-0.46 (0.42)
Minnesota	27	-0.48 (0.37)	West Virginia	27	1.24 (0.85)
Mississippi	19	1.1 (0.66)	Wisconsin	22	0.09 (0.44)
Missouri	23	-0.83 (0.43)	Wyoming	15	-0.36 (1.24)

° Figures in column represent OLS regression coefficients of challenger quality regressed on time and a constant. Standard Errors in parentheses. *** $p < 0.001$, ** $p < 0.01$, * $p < 0.05$, . $p < 0.10$

INDEX

Note: Page numbers in *italics* indicate figures, **bold** indicate tables in the text, and references following "n" refer endnotes.

Abramowitz, Alan 26
advertisements: candidate status for attribute *62*; television political advertisements 59
aggregate patterns 10, 20
Aldrich, John 11
ambition theory 11, 69
Arceneaux, K. 26, 39

Babbitt, Bruce 5
Babbitt, Paul 5
Banks, J. 28
Barnes, Tiffany D. 26, 38
Bartels, L. M. 117
Bianco, William T. 26
Biersack, Robert 26
Black, Gordon. 10, 68
Bond, J. R. 26, 31
Born, Richard 26
Branton, Regina P. 26, 38
the '*B*' Term 43–44
Buttice, Matthew K. 8, 29

cable: national cable networks 59; penetration 50, *50*, *52*
campaign communications decisions 59, 66
campaign costs 51, 53, 84–85; by candidate 49, *49*; *see also* costs

campaign finance laws 30
Campaign Media Analysis Group (CMAG) 59, 60
campaign theme 61
candidacy 9, 39–41
candidate emergence 10, 39
candidate quality 39; between 1972 and 2018 23; in open seat races 73–75
Canon, David T. 10, 28, 33, 34, 44–45, 80, 83
Carson, Jamie L. 9, 10, 12, 26, 31, 45–46
Cassese, Erin C. 26, 38
challenger quality 39; ambition theory 10–12; between 19th-century electoral politics 31; between 1946 and 1988 8; between 1972 and 2014 47; between 1972 and 2018 2–5; campaign finances 26; contemporary races 31; decline in 47, 94–98, 119–120; definition 7–9; dependent variable 84; dynamics by state 78, *78*; over time in contemporary elections 9–10; place *vs.* no limits by state (1972–2018) **71**, **73–75**; political experience 26; rational choice 10–12; states with limits *vs.* states without limits (1996–2018) **72**; strategic politicians and 12–13; trends in 10; U.S. House 33; U.S. Senate 26, 33
challengers: categories of 28; experienced 58–61, 63–66, 80, **81**, 85, **88**, 89, **90**,

91, **92**, **93**, 94, *96*, *101*, *102*, **104–105**; inexperienced 8, 58, 64–66, 118, 120, 121; spending 85–86, *95*, **97**, 99–101; *see also* challenger quality; strategic entries 38; voteshares 8, *8*
citizen legislatures 80, 91
communications strategies 3, 58; campaign 59, 61, 66; candidate categories 58
competitive expenditure levels 55, *55–57*
competitiveness 2, 3, 5, 23, 34, 38, 42, 43, 47, 56, 86, 87, 95, 98, 99, 120
comprehensive theory of candidacy 9
congressional elections 43, 44, 46, 59, 94, 111
congressional races 28
Cook, Timothy E. 26
corrupt, candidate characteristics 61, 65
costs: benefit calculations 11; campaign *51*, 57; television advertising 48, 49, *51*
Coutu, Mark 6
Covington, G. 26, 31
Cox, Gary W. 22, 26, 38, 109–116, 118n1
the 'C' Term 44

defeat incumbents 8, 58
Democratic challengers 4, 15, *15*, 16, 30, 91, 94, 119
Democratic incumbent 13, 39, 89, **90**, 91, **93**, 94, 95, 112
desirability of office 44
Desmarais, Bruce A. 26
dichotomous conceptualization 7, 26
discrete, forms of ambition 10, 68
dishonest, candidate characteristics 61, 65
district-level variables, challenger quality 33, 34, 42
Dugas, Mike 5
Dunaway, J. 39

elections: campaign costs 57; candidate quality in 10, 16, 25; challenger quality in 13; contemporary campaigns 6; contemporary congressional elections 10; invulnerable in contemporary congressional 5; probability of 11; procedures 30; U.S. House 26; U.S. Senate 16, *17*, 28, 29, 32
Erikson, Robert S. 109

Federal Election Commission 51, 53
filing deadlines 30; *see also* institutional factors

Flagstaff City Council 5
Fleisher, R. 26, 31
Fowler, Linda 9, 25, 29, 39, 42, 45, 46
Francis, Wayne L. 69
fundraising ability 25, 43

game theoretic analysis 28
Gelman, Andrew 112, 117
Green, Donald 26, 46
Green–Krasno formulation 29
Gronke, Paul 34, 38

Herrnson, Paul 26, 30, 58, 59
high-quality challengers 11; aggregate proportion of 17; incumbents' ads 64; probability 42, 45
honest, candidate characteristics 61, 63, 64
House challenger quality 16, 17

incumbency advantage 109–110; challenger quality and 110–111; direct components 111; indirect components 111; model 112–113; 1948–1990 period 113; quality effect 116–117; recent trends in 113–116; in U.S. House Elections (1974–2018) **114**, *115*
incumbents: communication strategies by opponent type *64*; communication strategy 63–65; facing experienced challengers 13, *14*; party strength 86, **97**, *98*; political characteristics of 32; reelection rates 6, *6*
institutional factors 30, 91–94
interactive model 101–107

Jacobson, Gary C. 8, 10, 12–14, 16, 18, 20, 25, 30, 31, 38, 46, 58, 85, 110, 114, 117
Johnson, M. 39

Katz, Jonathan N. 22, 26, 38, 109–116, 118n1
Kazee, Thomas A. 18
Kenney, Lawrence W. 69
Kernell, S. 13, 18, 38
Kiewiet, D.R. 28
King, Gary 112, 117
Kowl, Michael S. 26
Krasno, Jonathan S. 26, 46

La Raja, Raymond J. 26
legislative professionalization 45, 91, 93, 94

low-quality challengers 33, 55, 56, 61, 63–65, 118
Lublin, David Ian 29

Maisel, Sandy 6
majority status 86, 88, 89, 107
Matsui, Robert 5
McClure, Robert D. 45
Miller, Jeff 5
Moscardelli, Vincent G. 29

name recognition 25, 43
national economic conditions 32
national-level variables 42
national networks 59

open seats 18–21, *19–21*
organizational and coalition-building skills 25
ossified ruling clique 68

PAC contributions 54, *54*
party activism 26
party competition 78, 79, 80–81, 91–92; level of *79*, 80; two-party competition 45, 80
party rules, institutional factors 30
political action committees 53, 54
political ambition 10, 25, 68
political and social context 10
politically useful experience 26
political participation, conventional equation of 32
political party system 45, 121
political quality: of House challenger 16
political TV advertising 50, *52*
postwar elections 10, 14, 16, 43
post-Wesberry period 22
Powell, Richard 69
Praino, Rodrigo 29
pre-Wesberry period 22
probit analysis **87**, 88, **88**
professionalization: campaign execution professionalization 51; state legislative professionalization 45, 78–80, 82, 91
progressive, forms of ambition 10, 68
prudential exits 38
the '*p*' term 42–43
Pyeatt, Nicholas L. 26, 39

quality: conceptualization **27–28**; decline in 22–23, 119–120
quality challengers: emergence of 29, **35–37**; incumbents 31

quantities of interest 98–99
quasi-experimental design 69

Radanovich, George 5
Ragsdale, Lyn 26
Ranney, Austin 80
rational choice theory 32
re-election rates 6, 76, **76**, 111
Renzi, Rick 5
Republican challengers 4, 15, *15*, 16, 30, 91
Republican incumbent 89, **90**, **93**
retirement slumps 109
Rhode, David 10, 11, 68
Roberts, Jason 9, 10, 26, 31, 45, 46
Rush, Bobby 5

scare-off effect 111, *116*, 118n1
Schlesigner, Joseph 10, 68
sophomore surges 109
Sparks, Steven 26, 39
Squire, Peverill 25, 28, 29
state legislative elections: challenger quality in 32
state legislative professionalism *79*, 91
state legislative term limits 73–76, **76**, *79*, 87; structural/institutional variables 87
static, forms of ambition 10
stench of defeat 18
Stockemer, Daniel 29
Stone, Walter J. 8, 29
Stonecash, J.M. 110
strategic politicians thesis 12, 13, 29, 34
strategic voter theory 12
structural factors 30, 91–94

Talbert, J. C. 26
taxing 61, 62, 65
television: broadcast advertising on 48, 49, 57n1; costs 49, *50*, *51*, *60*; political advertisements 59
television advertisements 48–50, 59, 64; costs 48, 49, 51, *51*
Television Bureau of Advertising 49
term-limited legislators 72, 73

U.S. House elections: challenger quality in 70; challengers in 54; direct and indirect effects (scare-off and quality) in **116**, *116*; high-quality challengers in 75, 80; incumbency advantage in 110, **114**, *115*; incumbent party strength 107

U.S. Senate 16–18; between 1952 and 2000 29; experienced challengers 17, *17*, *18*; individual-level analysis of 32

Van Dunk, Emily 26
vanishing marginals 109
victory: incumbent's margin of 100, 108n2; lagged incumbent margin of **106**; probability of 39
voter: appeal 25; attention, broadcast media channels 32; gender bias from 39; House candidate quality, perceptions of 29; incumbent's contact 32
voteshares: challengers' average, 1972 and 2018 8; incumbent 109, 111; for incumbent's party 86

Wardingley, Raymond 5
Wesberry v. Sanders 22, 38
West, Darrell 48, 49, 59
Wielen, R. J. V. 39
Wilcox, Clyde 26
winning: probability of 33, 41–43; *see also* victory